Enjoy the
recipes!
xo
Carna Schade

the 90/10 life
COOKBOOK

HEALTHY FAMILY RECIPES, PRACTICAL TIPS & TASTY TREATS

GINA SCHADE
HEALTH & WELLNESS COACH

ISBN: 978-0-692-95419-5

This book is for entertainment purposes only. The information presented in this book is not meant to substitute for the advice of medical professionals. You are advised to consult with your physician regarding your family's nutrition, health, and well-being. The author is not responsible for any damage or negative consequence that may results from following the information in this book.

Written and published by: Gina Schade
Photographed by: Courtney Schultz (pages 5-27, 30-34, 44-45, 48, 56, 58, 86-90, 96, 109, 114, 122, 128-131, 138, 144, 150-153, 156-175), Gina Schade (pages 29, 36-42, 46, 52, 54, 60-84, 92, 98-104, 112, 116, 124, 126, 133, 136, 141-143, 146, 148), Anderson Photography (pages 28, 155) and Meg Esau (page 176)
All photographs edited by: Courtney Schultz (with the exception of pages 28, 52, 64, 68-69, 78, 124, 126, 148, 155, 176)
Graphic Design: Brittany Jaso
Editors: Sue Bollero Stack and Jeanna Leitch
Printed by: IngramSpark

Dedicated to...

My mom and dad for always pushing me to go for my dreams.

My husband Cody and sons Bode and Beckham for being my eternal taste-testers, honest critics, and loving supporters.

TABLE OF CONTENTS

Foreword

The first time I met Gina and heard her amazing, genuine laugh, I knew we were going to get along great. Little did I know at the time what an impact this feisty Italian would have on my life.

As someone who has been in relentless pursuit of having a healthy relationship with food, Gina and her realistic views on eating and wellness are a breath of fresh air. After years of doing the under-eating thing, the over eating thing, the protein only thing, and repeat, enough was enough. I wanted to enjoy food and have energy to live my life to the fullest, but there were still missing links: enter Gina. First off, Gina's passion for cooking—the way she truly finds joy in preparing foods that sustain and nourish—baffled me. Who wants to spend time in the kitchen? Gina! Her desire and delight to make healthy, tasty meals intrigued me.

As owner and instructor at B Present Studio, a boutique fitness studio specializing in providing a total mind-body-spirit experience, I am surrounded by (a few brave) men and (mostly) women who are seeking change. Many want to lose weight. Some have the working out routine in place, but consistently eating healthy, balanced meals is a different story. I knew I wanted to offer them more than a great workout. I also knew that working out alone would not be enough to help people get the results they wanted, and more importantly, live their best lives. That's when Gina and I started having conversations that ultimately came to the fruition of what is known today as the 21 Day Transformation.

The 21 Day Transformation is a comprehensive wellness program created and led by Gina. It includes a multitude of family-friendly recipes, online barre classes, accountability, encouragement, and a 90/10 food lifestyle approach. There are no gimmicks, fads, or magic pills—just real food recipes designed for real people who are seeking healthy, lasting change.

What has happened from the time I started cooking Gina's recipes until now is something I never would have seen coming—not only did I get exposed to many new ingredients, foods I never knew I liked, and unique flavor combinations, but I have also become someone who, even after a long day of work, wants to spend time in the kitchen. I never thought those words would leave my lips, let alone be demonstrated by my actions! Gina's recipes are the real deal! They're simple, easy to follow, filling, balanced, and they leave you feeling better than ever before. Her recipes have helped me to see that food prep doesn't have to be difficult, that I can cook, and even enjoy it!

Gina also knows that food is something we use to celebrate life events and share with family and friends. Her 90/10 approach to eating keeps me away from the extremism that always seemed to backfire. I am beyond grateful to Gina for this delicious assortment of go-to recipes and her impact on my newfound levels of food freedom. I know you are going to love her recipes too. I only hope someday you'll be able to hear her laugh, it really is the cherry on top!

Tammy Weisweaver

INTRODUCTION

I come from two large Italian families so, needless to say, I grew up with lots of kisses on the cheek, bowls of the best pasta you will ever eat, and an infinite amount of love. In our family, food has always been the way to the heart.

Growing up my friends would laugh and say that as soon as you walked into my house, my dad was there to offer you a steaming plate of baked mostaccioli—and you didn't dare refuse it! One of my favorite food memories is going to my Grandma Bollero's house, sitting around her kitchen table, and telling her about my day as she made me one of her world-famous toasted cheese sandwiches. Looking back, I think her two secret ingredients were massive amounts of butter and a serving size of love to match.

Today food is still very much tradition and an integral part of my family's life. Sundays are for sharing dinners and holidays are not complete without old family recipes like Thumbprints (page 154) and Million Dollar Fudge (page 168).

When I take a good hard look at what it is that I love about these recipes, it goes far beyond the taste. It is about how a simple recipe can bring everyone together around a table to share in laughter and love.

For years, I have been working to modify old, family favorite recipes into healthier versions so you can provide your family with delicious and nutritious meals. These recipes are proof that taste does not have to be sacrificed for health.

This cookbook is a collection of my most-loved, tried and true, easy to cook, healthy family recipes. And it wouldn't be the 90/10 Life without a few treats mixed into the bunch too.

My hope for you is that the meals in this cookbook inspire you to get your apron dirty and serve your family big heaping bowls of laughter and love.

xoxo,

Gina

Chapter 2
WHAT TO EXPECT

Pull up a chair, roll up your sleeves, and pour yourself a glass of wine. Let me share with you the meaning of the 90/10 Life and what you can expect from this cookbook.

First things first, the 90/10 Life:

90% on track, 10% off, because no one can be 100% all of the time.

What is life if you can't have a little fun?

I want you and your family to eat healthy most of the time, but I think leaving a little wiggle room for a piece of birthday cake, ice cream dates with your kids, or a dessert shared at the end of a date night with your spouse is important too. It isn't what you do once in awhile that matters; it's what you do most of the time.

The 90/10 Life is not a set calculation—it's a mindset. It is an understanding with yourself that if you allow your kids a Popsicle at the pool, it doesn't make you a bad parent. It's an understanding that if you enjoy a piece of cheesecake with your friends, it doesn't make you a failure. It means you do not attach shame or guilt to food choices. Living the 90/10 Life means you plan for and damn should enjoy a treat on occasion. Yes, I just said damn because you *can* enjoy your treats with such enthusiasm!

When it comes to 90% of your food choices, I want you to focus on fresh vegetables and fruit, lean and clean protein, healthy fats, and complex carbohydrates. Most of the recipes in this cookbook are designed to fall in the 90% category. When it comes to the 10%, I want you to choose treats that are homemade or are special to you.

I will be honest with you—I debated on whether or not I should share dessert recipes in this cookbook. After thinking it through, I realized that I wouldn't be being true to myself (or the 90/10 Life) if I didn't include the 10% recipes that I love! I am going to trust that you know you should be eating Chicken Cacciatore (page 94) for dinner and having Peanut Butter Crinkles (page 160) for a special treat—not vice versa.

THE RECIPES

This cookbook is a collection of the recipes that are closest to my heart. Many of the recipes are healthier versions of my childhood favorites. They are made from real food ingredients, are doable for parents with children at home, as well as empty-nesters, and will leave your loved ones begging for seconds!

The recipes do not exclude any of the macronutrients (protein, carbohydrates, and fat) and include all of the food groups. You will find tips and suggestions throughout the recipes to help you modify based on your family's needs and taste preferences. Cooking is truly an art. There is no right or wrong way to do it. Use my recipes exactly as is or feel free to spice them up any way you fancy...and get the family involved too!

THE 90/10 LIFE PRINCIPLES

The 90/10 Life Principles (page 17) are a collection of steps you can take to fully live out the 90/10 Life. The principles cover everything from food quality to mindset.

THE PANTRY

In a perfect world, all recipes would be cooked completely from scratch, but gone are the days of being able to spend all day in the kitchen. Practicing the 90/10 Life means you aren't afraid to take shortcuts when you can. You do not pass judgement on yourself if you buy a jar of spaghetti sauce instead of making your own. Chapter 4 is dedicated to helping you properly stock your pantry, refrigerator, and freezer with clean foods that will make healthy cooking easier for you. The goal is to spend less time at the stove and more time around the table with your family.

. . . .

I recommend you start with Chapter 3 and familiarize yourself with the 90/10 Life Principles. Next, take time to look over the information in Chapter 4. Take inventory of your pantry—are there things that need to be thrown out? Does it need to be organized? Do you need or want to purchase some of the recommended items? Then, thumb through all of the recipes and earmark the ones that speak to you. Lastly, tie up your apron and get cooking!

"The goal is to spend less time at the stove and more time around the table with your family."

THE 90/10 LIFE PRINCIPLES

EAT REAL, WHOLE FOODS

Whole foods are produced in nature and have not been refined or processed. They contain their original vitamin, mineral, and nutrient content. When you eat a whole food in its original form, the inherent nutrients synergistically work together to provide you with the ultimate platform for health. Examples of whole foods include vegetables, fruits, nuts, seeds, and whole grains.

FOOD QUALITY MATTERS

I recommend purchasing organic food when possible. The organic certification prohibits the use of specific, harmful herbicides and pesticides, bans genetically modified crops, requires outdoor access and pasture for livestock, prohibits the regular use of antibiotics and growth hormones, and requires farmers to use sustainable farming methods.[1] The best meat, seafood, and dairy come from animals raised in their natural environments (ideally organic) and fed their natural diets. Always look for words like "pasture-raised," "grass-fed," and "wild-caught." Organic and naturally raised food can be more expensive, but I encourage you to think of the money spent as your preventative health care dollars at work. The more you spend on your preventative health care now, the less you will spend on medical issues in the future.

ELIMINATE SCARY INGREDIENTS

"Scary ingredients" are ingredients that do not beneficially serve your body and have the potential to harm you. These ingredients are manufactured and do not exist in nature. They are generally added to a product during processing and include preservatives, flavor additives, artificial food dyes, artificial sugars, trans fats, and conventional vegetable oils.

BREAKUP WITH SUGAR

Sugar contributes to the development of multiple chronic conditions including obesity, type 2 diabetes, and heart disease. The American Heart Association recommends no more than 6-9 teaspoons (25-38 grams) of added sugar per day.[2] Added sugar is sugar that has been added to food during processing. This is different from natural sugar which is inherently found in a whole food. Many Americans are consuming well-beyond the recommended limit for added sugar per day. Added sugar can be found in yogurt, condiments, sauces, cereal, granola bars, and much more. There are multiple names for added sugar that can be listed on a label including corn syrup, fruit juice concentrate, invert sugar, high-fructose corn syrup, honey, maple syrup, brown rice syrup, agave, cane sugar, evaporated cane juice, sucrose, and more. I understand your 10% may include added sugar (mine does), but keep it out of your 90% as best you can—deal?

READ LABELS

The best way to determine if a product has "scary ingredients" or added sugar is to read the label. When you are reading labels, ask yourself the questions below. If you can answer yes to them, you likely have an acceptable product.

- Can I pronounce the ingredients?
- Do I know what the ingredients are?
- Would I cook with these ingredients in my own kitchen?
- Is this product free of hydrogenated or partially-hydrogenated oil (trans fat)?
- Is this product free of artificial sugars (aspartame, sucralose, saccharin, acesulfame potassium, neotame, and advantame)?
- Is this product free of artificial food dyes (FD&C Red No. 40, FD&C Yellow No. 5, etc.)?
- Is this product free of added sugar?
- Are the vegetable oils (corn/soy/canola) organic or non-GMO and expeller-pressed? (Expeller-pressing is a chemical-free process of oil extraction.)

COOK ONCE, EAT TWICE

This principle is the ultimate time saver. If you are going to spend time in your kitchen, you may as well get two meals for the time of one! How to make this principle work for you: 1. Double recipes so you have leftovers—enjoy them the following day or freeze for a later date. 2. Cook extra vegetables so you can have them as a side dish for lunch or scramble them into eggs. 3. Cook extra protein so you can top a salad with it.

BE PREPPY

It's all about the prep. You are more likely to choose a healthy food (like a vegetable) if it is already cleaned, washed, and chopped. As soon as you get home from the store, take time to wash, dry, and cut your produce. You will be thankful your food is prepped when it comes time for a snack or dinner.

GIVE YOURSELF GRACE

Learning to cook new meals, selecting new grocery products, and creating a healthy food lifestyle is a continual journey. If you make a mistake, buy the wrong ingredient, or burn a meal, give yourself grace instead of beating yourself up or throwing in the towel. Everything worthwhile takes time. The only way to learn is by experience.

MAKE FRIENDS WITH FOOD

Through my years of wellness coaching, I have found that many people have a negative association with food. In general, they think food will make them gain weight. They try to restrict calories to an all-time low, reduce portions, eliminate macronutrients, take weight loss supplements, and more. This does not result in a healthy body, mind, and spirit. Food is your friend! Food is to the body like gas is to a car. You need it to run. You don't need to eat less to be healthy, you just need to eat right. Think less about calories and more about quality.

TRUST YOUR BODY

Your body knows what it needs best. Give yourself extra nourishment on days you feel hungry, rest your body on days you are tired, exercise on days you are craving movement, and spend time with friends when you desire community. You will have more joy and peace in your life when you listen to your body.

Chapter 4

STOCK YOUR KITCHEN

A well-stocked pantry, refrigerator, and freezer is one of the keys to healthy cooking. When time is short or you forgot to turn on the slow cooker, a properly stocked kitchen allows you to create a meal on the fly.

PANTRY

Flours + Baking

almond flour
coconut flour
white whole wheat flour
whole wheat flour

allspice
baking powder
baking soda
cinnamon
dark chocolate chips
nutmeg
pure mint extract
pure vanilla extract

Grains

bread
brown or wild rice
quinoa
steel cut or rolled oats
tortillas
wraps

Sauces

enchilada sauce
pasta sauce
pesto
pizza sauce

Please see pages 24-26 for more specific product and brand recommendations.

Beans

black beans
chili beans
garbanzo beans
pinto beans
white beans

Jar or Can

artichokes
diced tomatoes
fire-roasted tomatoes
kalamata olives
roasted red peppers
salsa
tomato paste
tomato sauce

Snacks

crackers
jerky bars
snack bars
tortilla chips

Refrigerator

butter or ghee
cheese (block, string, or spreadable)
dairy or nut milk
eggs
fruit
lunch meat
protein (beef, pork, poultry, or seafood)
vegetables
yogurt

Nut / Legume / Seed Butters

almond butter
peanut butter
other nut or seed butters

Nuts + Seeds

almonds
cashews
hazelnuts
pecans
pistachios
walnuts

chia seeds
ground flaxseeds
hemp seeds
pumpkin seeds
sunflower seeds

Spices

basil
chili powder
cumin
coriander
dill
garlic powder
onion powder
oregano
paprika
parsley
red pepper flakes
rosemary
thyme

Condiments

BBQ sauce
coconut aminos
Dijon mustard
hot sauce
ketchup
mayonnaise
salad dressing
tamari sauce
yellow mustard
Worcestershire sauce

Oils + Vinegars

cold-pressed extra virgin olive oil
unrefined coconut oil
toasted sesame oil

apple cider vinegar
balsamic vinegar
red wine vinegar
white wine vinegar

Sweeteners

pure honey
pure maple syrup

Freezer

bean or vegetable burgers
frozen meals
fruit
protein (beef, pork, poultry, or seafood)
vegetables

TIPS

NUT/LEGUME/SEED BUTTERS | Avoid butters with hydrogenated oil and added sugar. A butter at its most basic level should include only the nut, legume (peanut), or seed from which it's derived. You may find there is a natural oil separation—do not be tempted to dump the oil, instead, gently stir it into the butter.

GRAINS | Select sprouted grains when possible. Sprouted grains are more easily digested than flour-based grains and will allow for better bioavailability of nutrients. Sprouted grain products may be found in the fresh bread section or the freezer section of your grocery store. Keep sprouted grains in the refrigerator or freezer to prolong shelf life.

Food for thought: A homemade bread calls for very minimal ingredients like flour, yeast, water, salt, oil, and sugar. Bread you purchase should have a similar ingredient list. Have you ever thought about why bakery bread goes bad in a few days but most of the bread in the grocery store can sit on the shelf for months?

NUTS & SEEDS | Look for unsalted, raw varieties. Some grocery stores will carry sprouted nuts—the same benefits as sprouted grains applies to sprouted nuts. It is best to store nuts in an opaque container in the refrigerator to protect them from light and heat damage.

OILS & VINEGARS | Olive oil is best for low to medium heat or as a finishing oil. Coconut oil is best for medium to high heat cooking. Toasted sesame oil is great as a finishing oil after your food has been removed from heat.

REFRIGERATOR | QUICK QUALITY KEY

> **EGGS/POULTRY/PORK:** organic (pasture-raised if possible) or antibiotic-free
> **BEEF/DAIRY:** organic (grass-fed if possible) or antibiotic and hormone-free
> **SEAFOOD:** wild-caught

Nitrates are a very common preservative added to breakfast and lunch meat. At minimum, look for varieties that are "uncured" or specify "no nitrates."

Plain yogurt varieties will not have any added sugar. If you do choose a sweetened variety, please compare labels and choose the one with the lowest amount of sugar (as long as there are no "scary ingredients").

My Favorite Brands

The following product recommendations are mostly free of "scary ingredients" at the time of writing this book. I only recommend products I cook with in my own kitchen and would serve my family. The food industry is always changing—it's important to frequently check food labels so you can continue to make informed decisions and purchases. See page 18 for label reading tips.

BEANS

CHILI BEANS | Westbrae Organic

NUT/LEGUME/SEED BUTTERS

ALMOND BUTTER | Justin's Classic, MaraNatha Organic Raw

PEANUT BUTTER | Aldi Simply Nature Organic Creamy, Justin's Classic, Smucker's Organic, Target Simply Balanced Organic, Whole Foods 365 Organic Unsweetened

OTHER | Nuttzo

CONDIMENTS

BBQ SAUCE | Annie's Organic Original (This is a low sugar BBQ sauce.)

COCONUT AMINOS | Bragg, Coconut Secret (Coconut aminos, made from coconut tree sap, are a gluten-free, lower sodium, and slightly sweet alternative to soy sauce.)

HOT SAUCE | Cholula Original, Frank's Original Red Hot Sauce, Tessemae's Mild or Hot Buffalo Sauce

KETCHUP | Annie's Organic, Heinz Organic, Whole Foods 365 Organic (Ketchup should be used sparingly as it is high in sugar.)

MAYONNAISE | Chosen Foods, Primal Kitchen, Sir Kensington's (Opt for avocado-based mayonnaise to increase your monounsaturated fat intake.)

SALAD DRESSING | Annie's, Bragg, Cindy's Kitchen, Hillary's, Primal Kitchen, Tessemae's (Select dressings with two grams of sugar or less per two tablespoon serving.)

TAMARI SAUCE | San-J Tamari Lite (Tamari sauce is a gluten-free alternative to soy sauce.)

GRAINS

SPROUTED BREAD | Angelic Bakehouse, Food for Life Ezekiel, Silver Hills

GLUTEN-FREE BREAD | Barely Bread, Food for Life Ezekiel, Simple Mills

OTHER BREAD | Breadsmith (100% Whole Wheat, Sourdough Whole Grain, Sourdough, Austrian Pumpernickel)

ENGLISH MUFFINS | Food for Life Ezekiel

TACO SHELLS | Food for Life Ezekiel, Whole Foods 365 Organic

WRAPS | Angelic Bakehouse, Engine 2, Food for Life Ezekiel, Julian's Bakery Paleo Wraps, Siete, Whole Foods 365 Organic

JAR OR CAN

DICED TOMATOES | Muir Glen Organic, San Marzano, Whole Foods 365 Organic

SALSA | Amy's, Aldi Simply Nature Organic, Frontera, Whole Foods 365 Organic

SAUCES

ENCHILADA | Frontera, Whole Foods 365 Organic, Simply Organic

PASTA | Aldi Simply Nature Organic, Mario Batali Organic, Rao's Homemade, Whole Foods 365 Organic

PESTO | Delallo Simply Pesto

PIZZA | Muir Glen Organic, Whole Foods 365 Organic

TOMATO | Muir Glen Organic, San Marzano, Whole Foods 365 Organic

SNACKS

CRACKERS | Back to Nature Multi-Seed Rice Thins (alternative to Wheat Thins), Doctor Kracker, Engine 2, Mary's Gone Crackers, Simple Mills, Way Better, Whole Foods 365 Woven Wheats (alternative to Triscuits)

JERKY BARS | Epic Bars

SNACK BARS | Larabars, RxBars, Simple Squares, That's It Bars

TORTILLA CHIPS | Frontera, Late July Restaurant Style Organic, Siete, Whole Foods 365 Organic

REFRIGERATOR

BACON | Applegate Natural and Organic, Whole Foods 365 Organic

BUTTER | Whole Foods 365 Organic, Organic Valley

CHEESE | Applegate Natural and Organic, Organic Creamery, Organic Valley, Whole Foods 365 Organic (Many pre-shredded cheeses are tossed in cellulose to prevent caking. Cellulose is derived from wood pulp—to avoid it, buy a block of cheese and grate it yourself for recipes that call for shredded cheese.)

EGGS | Eggland's Best Organic, Meijer True Goodness Organic, Organic Valley, Target Simply Balanced Organic, Whole Foods 365 Organic, Vital Farms Pasture-Raised

GHEE | Organic Valley

LUNCH MEAT | Applegate Natural and Organic, Plainville Natural and Organic, Whole Foods deli varieties

NUT MILK | Malk Unsweetened, New Barn Unsweetened

SAUSAGE | Applegate Natural and Organic, Bilinski's Natural and Organic, Brat Hans Antibiotic Free or Organic, Coleman's Natural and Organic

SWEETENED YOGURT | Siggi's 2% or 4% varieties, Stonyfield 100% Grass-fed Whole Milk Greek Vanilla Bean

UNSWEETENED YOGURT | Chobani Whole Milk Greek, Fage 2% Plain Greek, Nancy's Organic Whole Milk, Redwood Hills Farms Plain Goat Milk, Stonyfield 100% Grass-fed Whole Milk Plain, Stonyfield Organic Whole Milk Greek Plain, Stonyfield Organic Whole Milk Plain, Wallaby Organic Whole Milk Greek Plain, Wallaby Organic 2% Greek Plain

FREEZER

VEGETABLE OR BEAN BURGERS | Amy's, Dr. Praeger's, Hillary's, Don Lee Farms

FROZEN MEALS | Amy's, Blake's Organic, Dr. Praeger's, Red's Organic

Chapter 5

RECIPE FOR A HAPPY HOME

My Grandma Bollero had multiple copies of this recipe written down and tucked away in special places. After she passed, my mom handed down a copy to me so I could hang it in my kitchen. This is my all-time favorite recipe and I look to it daily as a reminder of the important things in life.

A Happy Home

4 C Love	5 spoons of Hope
2 C Loyalty	2 spoons of tenderness
3 C Forgiveness	4 qts. of Faith
1 C Friendship	1 Barrel of laughter

Take Love & Loyalty - mix thoroughly with Faith. Blend with tenderness, kindness and understanding. Add friendship and hope - sprinkle abundatly with laughter. Bake with sunshine. Serve daily with generous helpings.

Bena Bollero

CHAPTER 6
Shareables

Basic
CROSTINI

This is a classic crostini recipe that can be served with dips, on an antipasto tray, or used as a base for bruschetta.

INGREDIENTS

1 baguette loaf

1/8 cup olive oil

garlic salt, to taste

parsley, to taste

DIRECTIONS

Turn broiler on. Cut baguette into 1/2-inch slices. Place baguette slices on baking sheet. Brush both sides of slices with olive oil and lightly sprinkle with garlic salt and parsley. Broil for 1–2 minutes on each side or until slightly toasted.

serves eight

Stuffed PEPPADEW PEPPERS

My friend Angeline introduced me to Stuffed Peppadew Peppers. She and her husband Dominic invite us to their house every year for a dinner boat cruise on Shavehead Lake. This was one of the appetizers she served the first year we went. Cody and I were hooked at first bite and we now serve this as a staple appetizer when we entertain.

INGREDIENTS

20–25 peppadew peppers

5.2 oz. container
Boursin Garlic and Fine
Herbs Cheese

DIRECTIONS

Stuff a teaspoon-size amount of cheese into each peppadew pepper.

Tip: If you can't find peppadew peppers, you can substitute mini bell peppers.

serves four to six

Rustica
ANTIPASTO TRAY

Antipasto trays are a staple at our family celebrations and holidays. I love preparing antipasto trays when we entertain because they are versatile, easily customizable to the number of guests, and look beautiful. There is no right or wrong way to assemble one. Use your intuition and have fun with it!

INGREDIENTS

1 lb. Italian meat (salami, prosciutto, capocollo, mortadella)

1/2 lb. Italian hard cheese (Asiago or fontinella)

1/2 lb. Italian soft cheese (buffalo mozzarella, burrata, or ricotta)

1 cup marinated olives

Basic Crostini (page 32)

Stuffed Peppadew Peppers (page 33)

DIRECTIONS

Place ingredients on a large serving tray or wood cutting board.

If possible, source your ingredients from an Italian deli for maximum flavor and quality.

Short on time? Skip the Basic Crostini and Stuffed Peppadew Peppers and use crackers and already-marinated vegetables like roasted red peppers, artichokes, or mushrooms.

serves eight to ten

CREAM CHEESE & PEPPER JELLY

We have celebrated the Fourth of July in Boyne City, Michigan since I was a little girl. Every year, my mom makes a Cream Cheese and Pepper Jelly appetizer. We buy the pepper jelly from Mrs. Morrison's stand at the Farmer's Market in Boyne. I look forward to this appetizer all year long and the Fourth of July wouldn't be the same without it!

. . . .

INGREDIENTS

8 oz. block cream cheese

8 oz. pepper jelly

thin wheat or rice crackers, for serving

DIRECTIONS

Allow cream cheese to warm to room temperature. Spread cream cheese in a 9-inch pie plate. Evenly layer the pepper jelly on top of the cream cheese. Serve with crackers.

serves four to six

BRIE & PESTO *Bake*

This recipe is easy to whip up in a hurry. I like to keep a wheel of Brie and a jar of pesto on hand in my kitchen so I can make this when last minute plans pop up. It is creamy, decadent, and full of flavor.

INGREDIENTS

8 oz. Brie round

1/4 cup prepared pesto

Basic Crostini (page 32) or crackers, for serving

DIRECTIONS

Preheat oven to 350 degrees. Cut the rind off of the Brie as best as possible. (It doesn't need to be perfect.) Place Brie in a small baking dish. Evenly spread pesto on top of the Brie. Bake for 15 minutes or until Brie has melted and becomes bubbly. Let stand for 5 minutes. Serve with Basic Crostini or crackers.

serves four to six

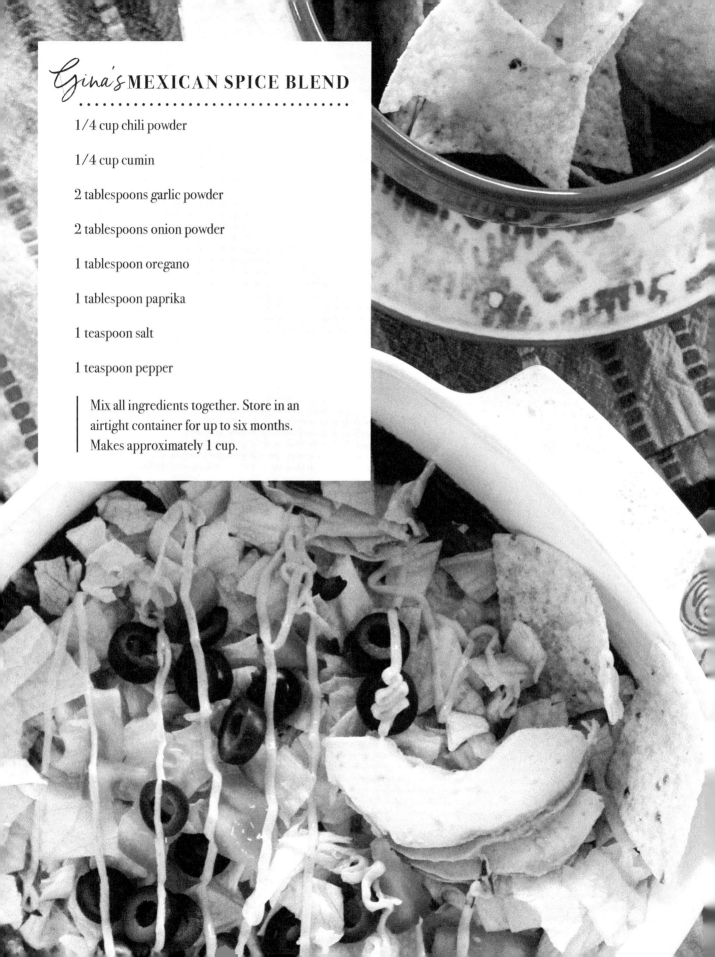

Gina's MEXICAN SPICE BLEND

1/4 cup chili powder

1/4 cup cumin

2 tablespoons garlic powder

2 tablespoons onion powder

1 tablespoon oregano

1 tablespoon paprika

1 teaspoon salt

1 teaspoon pepper

Mix all ingredients together. Store in an airtight container for up to six months. Makes approximately 1 cup.

Pepper Jack
BEAN DIP

This is a party favorite! It goes over great with both teenagers and adults. If you are serving a crowd, simply double the recipe and serve in a 9x11-inch baking dish. It can also be served as a side dish for Taco Tuesday. Who doesn't love a good bean dip with their tacos?

INGREDIENTS

15 oz. can refried beans

1 tablespoon Mexican seasoning (page 38)

1 1/2 cups pepper jack cheese, shredded

1 cup iceberg lettuce, shredded

1/2 cup tomato, diced

1/4 cup black olives, sliced

1-2 tablespoons chipotle mayonnaise, for drizzle

1 sandwich-size resealable bag

bell pepper slices or tortilla chips, for serving

salsa and sour cream, optional for serving

DIRECTIONS

Mix refried beans with seasoning. Spread beans on the bottom of a 7x7-inch baking dish. Top with pepper jack cheese, lettuce, tomato, and black olives. Snip one corner of the resealable bag. Put chipotle mayonnaise in the bag near the snipped corner. Squeeze the bag from the top down to push the mayonnaise out in a steady, even drizzle over the bean dip. (The smaller the snip, the thinner your line of mayonnaise will be.) Refrigerate for 2–4 hours before serving. Serve with bell pepper slices or chips.

Optional to serve salsa and sour cream on the side.

serves four to six

Mediterranean HUMMUS

This recipe takes basic hummus to the next level. It is a bit fancier for entertaining without being too difficult to make.

INGREDIENTS

10 oz. container plain or garlic hummus

2 cloves garlic, freshly minced

1 small sweet onion, chopped

1 cup roasted red bell peppers, chopped

1/3 cup Kalamata olives, sliced into thirds

1 tablespoon olive oil

1/3 cup feta cheese, crumbled

Basic Crostini (page 32), crackers, or vegetables, for serving

DIRECTIONS

Sauté onions and garlic in olive oil for 10 minutes or until onions are translucent. Add roasted red bell peppers and olives; continue to cook for 5-10 minutes. Remove from heat; let cool. Spread hummus in a 9-inch pie plate. Top hummus with sautéed vegetables and sprinkle with feta cheese. Serve with Basic Crostini (page 32), crackers, or vegetables.

serves six to eight

Buffalo CHICKEN DIP

This is hands down, the most-loved appetizer recipe in our circle of family and friends.
Trust me when I say that your loved ones will beg for the recipe when you make it for them!

INGREDIENTS

2 cups cooked chicken breast, shredded or diced

8 oz. block cream cheese

16 oz. sour cream

2 cups cheddar cheese, shredded

1/2 cup hot sauce

celery or tortilla chips, for serving

DIRECTIONS

Put all ingredients in a slow cooker and cook on low for 2–4 hours, stirring every 30 minutes. You may add extra hot sauce if you like a little heat! Serve with celery or tortilla chips.

In a hurry? Use rotisserie chicken instead of cooking your own.

serves four to six

CHAPTER 7
Breakfast

Italian
BREAKFAST CASSEROLE

This is Cody's favorite breakfast casserole. He loves the combination of pepperoni and Italian cheese, and he asks me to make it at least once a month. He takes the leftovers to work throughout the week for breakfast. Pepperoni may seem like an unusual ingredient for a breakfast casserole but it totally works!

INGREDIENTS

Immaculate Baking Company crescent rolls

10 eggs

1/2 cup dairy milk

12–16 pieces pepperoni (I use Applegate Farms.)

1 cup Italian cheese blend, shredded

1/4 teaspoon salt

1/8 teaspoon pepper

DIRECTIONS

Preheat oven to 350 degrees. Spread crescent rolls on the bottom of a greased 9x13-inch baking dish. Layer pepperoni and cheese on top of the crescent rolls.

In a mixing bowl, beat eggs with a fork. Add milk, salt, and pepper; whisk together. Pour egg mixture over pepperoni and cheese. Bake at 350 degrees for 45–60 minutes or until a fork inserted comes out clean.

 *serves eight*

Kale, Bacon & Goat Cheese
BREAKFAST CASSEROLE

This is a great casserole to make for brunch with friends, a shower, or a special event.
The ingredients are slightly upscale but it has an approachable flavor that everyone loves.

INGREDIENTS

Immaculate Baking Company crescent rolls

10 eggs

1/2 cup dairy milk

1 lb. bacon, cooked and crumbled

1 cup goat cheese, crumbled

1 cup kale, finely shredded

1/4 teaspoon salt

1/8 teaspoon pepper

DIRECTIONS

Preheat oven to 350 degrees. Spread crescent rolls on the bottom of a greased 9x13-inch baking dish. Layer kale, bacon, and goat cheese on top of the crescent rolls.

In a mixing bowl, beat eggs with a fork. Add milk, salt, and pepper; whisk together. Pour egg mixture over bacon, goat cheese, and kale. If kale pops above the egg mixture, gently press it down with a fork. This will prevent exposed kale from crisping on the top. Bake at 350 degrees for 45–60 minutes or until a fork inserted comes out clean.

serves eight

Mom's Classic
BREAKFAST CASSEROLE

My mom has been making versions of this breakfast casserole for years. We spend Thanksgiving together at our family cabin and this is always on the menu. It reminds me of sitting around the cabin table, drinking coffee, laughing, and eating breakfast with my family.

INGREDIENTS

3 cups baking potatoes, diced

10 eggs

1/2 cup dairy milk

2 cups ham, shredded or diced

1 cup sharp cheddar cheese, shredded

1/2 cup green onion, finely sliced

1/4 teaspoon salt

1/8 teaspoon pepper

DIRECTIONS

Preheat oven to 350 degrees. Spread potatoes on the bottom of a greased 9x13-inch baking dish. Layer ham, cheese, and green onion on top of the potatoes.

In a mixing bowl, beat eggs with a fork. Add milk, salt, and pepper; whisk together. Pour egg mixture over ham, cheese, and green onion. Bake at 350 degrees for 45–60 minutes or until a fork inserted comes out clean.

 *serves eight*

Beckham's
BREAKFAST SCRAMBLE

I wrote this cookbook while pregnant with our second son, Beckham. I craved this breakfast almost every single morning of my first trimester. I won't be surprised if he grows up to be an avocado, bacon, and cheese loving little boy!

INGREDIENTS

8 eggs

1/4 cup dairy milk

1 cup sharp cheddar cheese, shredded

1/2 lb. bacon, cooked and crumbled

1 tablespoon butter

1/4 teaspoon salt

1/8 teaspoon pepper

1 avocado, sliced

DIRECTIONS

Whisk eggs, milk, salt, and pepper together. Heat butter over medium heat; swirl pan to coat. Place bacon in bottom of pan. Pour egg mixture over bacon. Scramble eggs. A few minutes before eggs are set, add cheddar cheese. Top scrambled eggs with sliced avocado.

serves four

Five-Ingredient
CRUSTLESS QUICHE

This quiche is a great grain-free and low-carb breakfast option. I frequently make this and eat a piece throughout the week for breakfast.

INGREDIENTS

10 eggs

1 cup broccoli, roughly chopped

1/2 cup grape tomatoes, sliced in half

1/2 cup feta cheese, crumbled

1/2 lb. bacon, cooked and crumbled

1/4 teaspoon salt

1/8 teaspoon pepper

DIRECTIONS

Preheat oven to 350 degrees. In a mixing bowl, beat eggs with a fork. Add broccoli, grape tomatoes, feta, bacon, salt, and pepper to eggs; mix well.

Pour egg mixture into a greased 9-inch pie plate. Bake for 30 minutes or until a fork inserted comes out clean.

 serves six

AVOCADO TOAST
five ways

This is one of my favorite breakfast recipes. It is easy and filling!
My favorite toppings are chipotle mayonnaise and red pepper flakes.

INGREDIENTS

1/2 avocado, pit and skin removed

1 piece of bread, toasted

salt, to taste

Optional toppings:

fried egg

fried egg and cooked bacon

chipotle mayonnaise and red pepper flakes

scrambled egg and salsa

cucumber and tomato slices

DIRECTIONS

Gently mash avocado. Top toast with mashed avocado and sprinkle with salt. Enjoy as is or add optional toppings.

serves one

Most-Loved
BLUEBERRY BAKED OATMEAL

This recipe is slightly modified from one given to me by my Aunt Sue—we share a love for baked oatmeal. I like to serve mine warmed in a bowl with sliced banana and a splash of warm milk.

INGREDIENTS

3 cups old-fashioned rolled oats

1 cup blueberries

2 eggs

1 cup dairy or nut milk

1/4 cup unsweetened applesauce

1/2 cup brown sugar

1 teaspoon salt

1 teaspoon cinnamon

DIRECTIONS

Preheat oven to 350 degrees. Thoroughly mix eggs, milk, applesauce, brown sugar, salt, and cinnamon. Stir in oats and blueberries. Pour into a greased 9-inch pie plate. Bake for 25 minutes or until a fork inserted comes out clean.

serves six

Rustic
YOGURT
PARFAIT
three ways

This is a great breakfast to make ahead and grab on the run. Get creative and experiment with your own fruit and nut combinations!

· ·

INGREDIENTS

1 cup yogurt

1 mason jar

Toppings:

one cup of berries & 1/4 cup sliced almonds

one diced peach & 1/4 cup chopped pecans

one small sliced banana & 1/4 cup chopped walnuts

DIRECTIONS

Layer the ingredients in the mason jar in the following order: 1/2 cup yogurt, 1/2 of the fruit, 1/2 of the nuts, 1/2 cup yogurt, 1/2 of the fruit, 1/2 of the nuts. Put lid on and refrigerate until ready to enjoy.

serves one

The FUNKY MONKEY

This is my preferred breakfast before working out. The complex carbohydrates from the bread and banana provide me with stable energy and the fat and protein from the peanut butter keep me satisfied until I have time to sit down for a larger meal. Plus, it's easy, quick, and delicious. You can create a "toast bar" and set out bowls of bananas, nut butters, dark chocolate chips, shredded coconut, and more to let your kids build their own toast.

INGREDIENTS

1 piece of bread, toasted

2 tablespoons peanut butter

1/2 banana, sliced

cinnamon, to taste

Optional toppings:

dark chocolate chips (I use Enjoy Life.)

shredded coconut

strawberries

DIRECTIONS

Top toast with peanut butter and sliced banana. Sprinkle with cinnamon. Add optional toppings if desired.

 serves one

Pumpkin
CHOCOLATE CHIP MUFFINS

This recipe is modified from an original version given to me by my mother-in-law, Robin. She made these for Cody growing up. He still loves them to this day and they have become a favorite in our home. You can swap walnuts or pecans for the chocolate chips if you prefer but a little chocolate for breakfast never hurt anyone!

INGREDIENTS

15 oz. can 100% pure pumpkin

3 cups white whole wheat flour

1 1/2 cups coconut sugar

1 cup dark chocolate chips (I use Enjoy Life.)

1/2 cup unsweetened applesauce

2/3 cup water

3 eggs

2 teaspoons baking soda

1/2 teaspoon salt

1 teaspoon cinnamon

1 teaspoon nutmeg

DIRECTIONS

Preheat oven to 350 degrees. In a bowl, mix flour, baking soda, salt, cinnamon, and nutmeg together; set aside. With a mixer, mix sugar, applesauce, water, and eggs together. Mix pumpkin into sugar mixture. Add flour mixture one cup at a time to sugar mixture; mix until well-combined. Stir in chocolate chips. Fill greased muffins tins 1/2 of the way full. Bake for 20–25 minutes or until a fork inserted comes out clean.

makes 24 muffins

Cinnamon Raisin
FRENCH TOAST

This recipe reminds me of my Grandma Simeri. When we were kids she was brave enough to have all of the girl cousins spend the night at once. We would get to stay up late, watch movies, eat junk food, and all pile into her bed at the end of the night. In the morning, we would sit around her kitchen table and she would make us batches of French toast. It felt so special as a kid and is one of my favorite food memories.

INGREDIENTS

8 pieces cinnamon raisin bread (I use Food for Life Ezekiel.)

4 eggs

1/4 cup dairy or nut milk

2 teaspoons vanilla extract

2 teaspoons cinnamon

2 tablespoons butter

butter and pure maple syrup, for serving

Optional toppings:

bananas (my favorite)

blueberries

nuts

powdered sugar

peanut butter (Cody's favorite)

DIRECTIONS

Whisk eggs, milk, vanilla, and cinnamon together in a flat dish. Heat 1/2 tablespoon butter over medium heat. Dip two pieces of bread in egg mixture and place in skillet. Cook for 3–5 minutes on each side or until slightly browned. Heat another 1/2 tablespoon of butter and cook two additional pieces of dipped bread. Continue this pattern until all bread is cooked. Serve with butter, pure maple syrup, and optional toppings if desired.

serves four

Simple
BLUEBERRY BANANA PANCAKES

This is a great grain-free pancake recipe. It is easy to make and calls for minimal ingredients. You will love the combination of bananas and blueberries together—so delicious.

INGREDIENTS

4 medium or 3 large ripe bananas, mashed

1 cup blueberries

4 eggs

2 tablespoons coconut flour

2 teaspoons cinnamon

2 teaspoons vanilla extract

1 tablespoon butter

butter and pure maple syrup, for serving

DIRECTIONS

Mix bananas, eggs, coconut flour, vanilla, and cinnamon together. Gently mix in blueberries. Heat 1/2 tablespoon butter over medium heat. Pour half of the batter into four evenly sized pancakes. Cook 2–4 minutes on each side or until slightly browned. Heat the remaining butter and cook the second batch of pancakes. Serve with butter and pure maple syrup.

serves four

Rustic
PUMPKIN PANCAKES

This is one of my family's favorite fall breakfasts. The cinnamon, nutmeg, and pumpkin combination is perfect for the season. I love serving these to my family on cool, fall Sundays when we can sleep in and enjoy a long breakfast together.

INGREDIENTS

1 cup white whole wheat flour

1/2 cup 100% pure pumpkin

1 egg

1 cup dairy or nut milk

1/2 teaspoon vanilla

1 teaspoon cinnamon

1/4 teaspoon nutmeg

2 tablespoons coconut sugar

1 teaspoon baking powder

1/4 teaspoon salt

1 tablespoon butter

butter and pure maple syrup, for serving

DIRECTIONS

Combine flour, baking powder, salt, cinnamon, nutmeg, and sugar in large bowl. Whisk pumpkin and egg together in a medium bowl. Add milk and vanilla to pumpkin mixture; whisk until smooth. Pour wet ingredients over the dry ingredients and fold until just combined. A few lumps will remain. Heat 1/2 tablespoon butter and pour half of the batter into four evenly sized pancakes. Cook 2–4 minutes on each side or until slightly browned. Heat the remaining butter and cook the second batch of pancakes. Serve with butter and pure maple syrup.

Tip: For a treat, stir in 1/4 cup mini dark chocolate chips.

serves four

CHAPTER 8
Salads + Sandwiches

Salads and sandwich recipes are written to serve four but if you are whipping up a salad or sandwich for one, simply add the desired amount of ingredients to a bowl or bread and enjoy!

 Mom's
CHICKEN SALAD

My mom always whipped up chicken salad for us as kids. This was one of her go-to combinations. Don't get thrown off by the pickle relish—it seems like an odd ingredient but it totally works!

INGREDIENTS

1 lb. chicken breast

1/3 cup mayonnaise

1/3 cup dried cranberries

1/3 cup walnut pieces

1/8 cup pickle relish

1/4 teaspoon salt

1/8 teaspoon pepper

celery, cucumbers, lettuce wraps, or crackers, for serving

DIRECTIONS

Preheat oven to 400 degrees. Place chicken in a greased baking dish. Bake for 25–40 minutes or until chicken reaches an internal temperature of 165 degrees. Let chicken cool; dice into small pieces and place in a bowl. Add mayonnaise, dried cranberries, walnut pieces, pickle relish, salt, and pepper; stir to combine. Serve with celery, cucumbers, lettuce wraps, or crackers.

 serves four

Cody's
CHICKEN SALAD

This is Cody's favorite chicken salad. The first time I made it for him he raved about it. It has become a staple in our household and I frequently make it for him to take to work for lunch.

INGREDIENTS

1 lb. chicken breast

1/3 cup mayonnaise

1/4 cup raisins

1/4 cup celery, sliced

1/4 cup almonds, sliced or slivered

1/4 teaspoon salt

1/8 teaspoon pepper

celery, cucumbers, lettuce wraps, or crackers, for serving

DIRECTIONS

Preheat oven to 400 degrees. Place chicken in a greased baking dish. Bake for 25–40 minutes or until chicken reaches an internal temperature of 165 degrees. Let chicken cool; dice into small pieces and place in a bowl. Add mayonnaise, raisins, celery, almonds, salt, and pepper; stir to combine. Serve with celery, cucumbers, lettuce wraps, or crackers.

serves four

Chipotle
CHICKEN SALAD

This is a fun twist on a basic chicken salad. The chipotle mayonnaise gives the salad a little extra zip. I often make a big batch of this on Sundays and Cody and I enjoy it throughout the week for lunches. I like mine folded into lettuce wraps and Cody prefers his with crackers or tortilla chips.

INGREDIENTS

1 lb. chicken breast

1 tablespoon Mexican seasoning (page 38)

1/3 cup chipotle mayonnaise

1/8 cup green onion, sliced

1/8 teaspoon salt

avocado, for serving

feta, for serving

red onion, for serving

celery, cucumbers, lettuce wraps, crackers, or tortilla chips, for serving

DIRECTIONS

Preheat oven to 400 degrees. Place chicken in a greased baking dish. Season chicken with Mexican seasoning. Bake for 25–40 minutes or until chicken reaches an internal temperature of 165 degrees. Let chicken cool; dice into small pieces and place in a bowl. Add chipotle mayonnaise, green onion, and salt; stir to combine. Top with avocado, feta, and red onion. Serve with celery, cucumbers, lettuce wraps, crackers, or tortilla chips.

serves four

Seven Layer SALAD

This recipe reminds me of my mother-in-law, Robin. She makes a version of this for special celebrations and holidays. Traditional seven layer salad recipes call for a dressing mixture of miracle whip and sugar—I prefer serving mine with ranch or a more savory dressing to remove a majority of the sugar.

INGREDIENTS

2–3 heads of Romaine lettuce, chopped

1 lb. bacon, cooked and crumbled

8 hard-boiled eggs, diced

1 cup grape tomatoes, sliced in half

1 cup cheddar cheese, shredded

1 cup frozen peas, thawed

1/4 cup or more red onion, finely diced

1 avocado, diced

freshly cracked black pepper, to taste

ranch dressing, for serving

DIRECTIONS

Layer Romaine, bacon, eggs, grape tomatoes, cheddar cheese, frozen peas, and red onion in a large glass bowl. Season with freshly cracked black pepper. Before serving, add diced avocado to salad. Drizzle ranch dressing over the top of the salad. Using tongs, mix salad ingredients together.

serves four

Greek SALAD

This is a great, classic Greek salad. It is flavorful and filling. If you are serving this alongside of a main dish, you can omit the chicken and build it with just the vegetables and cheese—it is delicious both ways!

INGREDIENTS

1 lb. chicken breast

1 1/2 teaspoons parsley

1/2 teaspoon oregano

1/8 teaspoon salt

1/8 teaspoon pepper

1/2 lemon, for squeezing

2–3 heads of Romaine lettuce, chopped

1/2 cup grape tomatoes, sliced in half

1/2 cup cucumbers, diced

1/2 cup feta cheese, crumbled

1/8 cup red onion, finely diced

4 pepperoncini peppers

freshly cracked black pepper, to taste

dressing of choice, for serving (I use Primal Kitchen Greek.)

DIRECTIONS

Preheat oven to 400 degrees. Place chicken in a greased baking dish. Season with parsley, oregano, salt, and pepper. Bake for 25–40 minutes or until chicken reaches an internal temperature of 165 degrees. Let chicken cool; dice into small pieces and set aside. Squeeze fresh lemon juice over diced chicken.

Place Romaine in a large serving bowl. Top with grape tomatoes, cucumber, feta cheese, red onion, and chicken. Season with freshly cracked black pepper. Drizzle dressing of choice over the top of the salad. Garnish with pepperoncini peppers.

serves four

Southwest SALAD

This is my all-time favorite salad recipe. The combination of complex carbohydrates, protein, and fat is super filling and the flavors are bold! I could eat this every day!

INGREDIENTS

1 lb. chicken breast

1 tablespoon Mexican seasoning (page 38)

2–3 heads of Romaine lettuce, chopped

1/2 cup corn

1/2 cup black beans

1/2 cup tomato, diced

1 avocado, diced

1/2 cup feta cheese, crumbled (may use cheddar or pepper jack)

8 tortilla chips, gently crushed

sour cream, for serving

salsa, for serving

DIRECTIONS

Preheat oven to 400 degrees. Place chicken in a greased baking dish. Season with Mexican seasoning. Bake for 25–40 minutes or until chicken reaches an internal temperature of 165 degrees. Let chicken cool; dice into small pieces and set aside.

Place Romaine in a large serving bowl. Top with corn, black beans, tomato, avocado, cheese, chicken, and tortilla chips. Use salsa and sour cream as your dressing. A jalapeño ranch, chipotle ranch, or chili lime vinaigrette dressing would also compliment this salad well.

serves four

Peachy Keen
SPINACH SALAD

This is a refreshing salad for warm summer days! It is a great dish to bring to a party, get-together, or girls' night.

INGREDIENTS

12 cups fresh spinach leaves

4 peaches, pit removed and diced

3/4 cup goat cheese, crumbled

1/2 cup pecans, roughly chopped

freshly cracked black pepper, to taste

dressing of choice, for serving
(I use Tessemae's Honey Balsamic.)

DIRECTIONS

Place spinach in a large serving bowl. Top with peaches, goat cheese, and pecans. Season with freshly cracked black pepper. Drizzle dressing of choice over the top of the salad.

serves four

Mediterranean
PITA POCKETS

INGREDIENTS

1 lb. chicken breast

1 1/2 teaspoons parsley

1/2 teaspoon oregano

1/8 teaspoon salt

1/8 teaspoon pepper

1/2 lemon, for squeezing

4 pita pockets

1 cup lettuce

1/2 cup hummus

1/2 cup roasted red peppers, diced

1/2 cup feta cheese, crumbled

DIRECTIONS

Preheat oven to 400 degrees. Place chicken in a greased baking dish. Season with parsley, oregano, salt, and pepper. Bake for 25–40 minutes or until chicken reaches an internal temperature of 165 degrees. Let chicken cool; dice into small pieces and set aside. Squeeze lemon juice over diced chicken.

Spread two tablespoons of hummus inside of each pita pocket. Stuff each pita pocket with 1/2 cup chicken, 1/4 cup lettuce, 1/8 cup roasted red peppers, and an 1/8 cup feta cheese.

 serves four

Italian Stallion
WRAPS

Every once in awhile, there isn't anything that satisfies quite like a salami sandwich. When I was a little girl, my Grandma and Grandpa Bollero always had Italian salami, cheese, and bread in their kitchen. My Grandma would hide a few pieces of salami for me in the back of their refrigerator so she could always make me a sandwich when I came over. This is my "adult version" of the salami and cheese sandwich I loved so much as a kid.

INGREDIENTS

4 wraps (I use Angelic Bakehouse or Food for Life Ezekiel)

8 tablespoons cream cheese

12 pieces salami, sliced thin

8 pieces turkey breast, sliced thin

1 cup lettuce, finely shredded

1/4 cup tomato, finely diced

1 tablespoon red onion, finely diced

1 tablespoon Italian dressing

DIRECTIONS

Lay wraps flat. Spread two tablespoons of cream cheese over each wrap. In a small mixing bowl, combine lettuce, tomato, red onion, and Italian dressing together. Evenly layer salami, turkey, and lettuce mixture over each wrap; roll wrap.

serves four

Classic Club
ENGLISH MUFFIN ROUNDS

This is a fun twist on a classic club sandwich. Kids (and adults) will find it fun to eat their sandwiches open-face style on English muffins. You can take this concept and try it with your family's favorite sandwich combinations!

INGREDIENTS

4 English muffins (I use Food for Life Ezekiel.)

8 pieces bacon, cooked and broken in half

4 pieces ham, sliced thin

4 pieces turkey, sliced thin

4 slices cheddar cheese

2 tablespoons mayonnaise

1 tablespoon yellow mustard

4 pieces leaf lettuce

4, 1/2-inch thick tomato slices

1/2 tablespoon butter, melted

DIRECTIONS

Turn broiler on. Break English muffins apart and lay on a baking sheet. Brush both sides of English muffins with butter. Broil for 1–2 minutes or until English muffins become just slightly browned; remove from oven. Evenly spread mayonnaise and mustard over English muffin halves. Top each half with the ingredients in the following order: lettuce, tomato, turkey, ham, bacon, and cheese. You may need to fold ham and turkey depending on size. Put English muffins back into oven and broil for 2–3 minutes or until ingredients are warmed and cheese has melted. (If you prefer, you can leave lettuce and tomato off until after broiling. This will allow for vegetables to stay crisp.)

serves four

CHAPTER 9
Dinner

Mom's Homemade
PASTA SAUCE

The smell of Mom's Homemade Pasta Sauce cooking on the stovetop brings me back to childhood. I grew up eating this sauce and it is my ultimate comfort food. There is something so special, empowering, and nostalgic about making a homemade batch of sauce. It is much easier than you think it would be—give it a try some Sunday when you have time to let it simmer all day on the stove. I like to make double batches and freeze half so I always have some available.

INGREDIENTS

1 small onion, chopped

1/2 teaspoon garlic, minced

28 oz. can crushed tomatoes

1/2 cup water

2 tablespoons olive oil

1 teaspoon salt

2 teaspoons basil

1 teaspoon oregano

1 teaspoon parsley

1/2 teaspoon pepper

2 teaspoons brown sugar

DIRECTIONS

Heat olive oil over medium heat in a large sauce pan. Sauté onion and garlic in olive oil for 8–10 minutes or until soft. Add all of the other ingredients and simmer for 30–60 minutes or longer. The longer you simmer, the more the flavor develops.

Make it a meat sauce: Add one pound of Italian sausage to the onion and garlic; omit the salt. Cook and crumble until sausage is cooked throughout. Do not drain the fat—it adds a lot of flavor!

serves four

Mom's Homemade
ITALIAN MEATBALLS

Spaghetti and meatballs was a standard meal growing up in our household. Mom's Homemade Italian Meatballs recipe can't be beat! I like to serve my meatballs over spaghetti squash but they can also be served more traditionally over pasta or used for meatball sandwiches.

INGREDIENTS

3/4 lb. ground chuck

1/4 lb. ground pork

3/4 cup Parmesan or Romano cheese, grated

3/4 cup coarse ground breadcrumbs from dry Italian bread

2 large eggs

2 tablespoons parsley

1/4 teaspoon garlic powder

1 teaspoon salt

1/2 teaspoon pepper

Mom's Homemade Pasta Sauce (page 89) or 1 jar of pasta sauce

DIRECTIONS

Preheat oven to 300 degrees. Mix all ingredients together (except for Mom's Homemade Pasta Sauce) and roll into 8–12 meatballs. Place on a greased baking sheet and bake for 30 minutes or until cooked throughout, turning once. Warm sauce over stovetop. Place cooked meatballs in sauce.

Serving Suggestion: Serve over Basic Spaghetti Squash (page 135).

serves four

Oven-Baked
CHICKEN PARMESAN

Cody and I would both say that this is one of our favorite meals. It is our go-to option when we have friends and family over for dinner. It is foolproof, quick to cook, and impresses guests. Because it is lightly coated with bread crumbs and baked in the oven vs. heavily breaded and fried, it is a much healthier version than what you will find in a restaurant.

INGREDIENTS

1 1/2 lbs. chicken breast, divided into four equal pieces

1 cup pasta sauce

4 slices Swiss cheese

1 cup Italian-seasoned bread crumbs

1/4 cup Parmesan cheese, grated or shredded

2 eggs, whisked

1/8 teaspoon salt

1/8 teaspoon pepper

DIRECTIONS

Preheat oven to 400 degrees. Season chicken with salt and pepper. Place whisked eggs in a flat dish. Mix breadcrumbs and Parmesan cheese together and place in a secondary flat dish. Dip each piece of chicken in egg and gently press each side of the chicken into breadcrumb mixture. Place chicken in a greased baking dish and bake, uncovered, for 25–40 minutes or until chicken reaches an internal temperature of 165 degrees. Remove chicken from the oven and put 1/4 cup sauce over each piece. Layer one piece of cheese over the sauce. Turn oven to broil. Broil for 2–3 minutes or until cheese is bubbly and slightly browned.

Serving Suggestion: Serve over Basic Spaghetti Squash (page 135) or with Lemon Parmesan Asparagus (page 151).

serves four

Mom's Easy
CHICKEN CACCIATORE

This is another favorite recipe of mine...I guess I could call it comfort food! It is flavorful, easy to make, and packed with vegetables. It was the first meal I requested after bringing our son Bode home from the hospital. It is one of those recipes the whole family will love. I enjoy cooking this on Sundays for my family.

INGREDIENTS

1 lb. chicken breast, cut into medium size pieces

1 sweet onion, chopped

4 garlic cloves, minced

1 summer squash, chopped

3/4 cup roasted red bell peppers, sliced

2 large portobello mushrooms, de-stemmed and sliced

1 zucchini, chopped

2 tablespoons olive oil

Mom's Homemade Pasta Sauce (page 89) or 1 jar of pasta sauce

1 tablespoon Italian seasoning

1/4 teaspoon salt

1/8 teaspoon pepper

Parmesan cheese, for serving

DIRECTIONS

Preheat oven to 200 degrees. Heat olive oil over medium heat. Sauté onion, garlic, squash, roasted red bell peppers, mushrooms, and zucchini for 15–20 minutes or until tender. Season with Italian seasoning, salt, and pepper. Transfer vegetables to a greased baking dish. Add chicken breast pieces and entire jar of pasta sauce to baking dish. Cover with foil and bake for 3.5 hours. Chicken should reach an internal temperature of 165 degrees. Before serving, sprinkle with shaved Parmesan cheese.

Serving Suggestion: Serve over Basic Spaghetti Squash (page 135).

serves four

Slow Cooker
SAUSAGE & PEPPERS

Sausage and peppers reminds me of my dad. They are a regular part of his recipe rotation and he almost always makes them for extended family holidays. This recipe is a quick and simple version that doesn't skimp on taste. There is nothing better than being able to throw ingredients into a slow cooker and coming home to a meal that everybody loves.

INGREDIENTS

4 mild Italian sausage links

1 sweet onion, sliced

1 red bell pepper, sliced

2 green bell peppers, sliced

Mom's Homemade Pasta Sauce (page 89) or 1 jar of pasta sauce

1 tablespoon Italian seasoning

DIRECTIONS

Put all ingredients in a greased slow cooker and cook on low for 8–10 hours.

Serving Suggestion: Serve over Basic Spaghetti Squash (page 135) or on crusty Italian buns.

serves four

Baked
PESTO CHICKEN

This is an easy, quick, and delicious recipe. It literally takes
one minute to whip up before putting it into the oven!

INGREDIENTS

1 1/2 lbs. chicken breast, divided into
four equal pieces

1/2 cup pesto

1 cup mozzarella cheese, shredded

1/4 teaspoon salt

1/8 teaspoon pepper

DIRECTIONS

Preheat oven to 350 degrees. Place chicken in a
greased baking dish. Season with salt and pepper.
Spread two tablespoons of pesto onto each portion
of chicken breast. Cover baking dish with foil and
cook for 45–60 minutes or until chicken reaches an
internal temperature of 165 degrees. Remove chicken
from oven. Turn oven to broil. Sprinkle chicken with
mozzarella cheese and broil for 2–3 minutes or until
cheese becomes browned and bubbly.

Serving Suggestion: Serve over Basic Pesto Zoodles
(page 135) or Garlic Mashed Cauliflower (page 137).

serves four

Portobello Mushroom
PIZZAS

Serving traditional pizza toppings on portobello mushrooms is a grain-free and low-carb
way to enjoy pizza. Make the recipe as is or play around with your favorite pizza toppings.

INGREDIENTS

8 large portobello mushrooms, stems removed

1/2 lb. ground Italian sausage, cooked
and crumbled

1/2 small sweet onion, diced

1/2 cup roasted red bell peppers, diced

1/4 cup Kalamata olives, pitted and sliced in half

2 garlic cloves, minced

1 1/2 cups mozzarella cheese, shredded

1/2 cup feta cheese, crumbled

1 1/2 cups pizza sauce

2 tablespoons olive oil, divided

1 teaspoon Italian seasoning

1/4 teaspoon garlic powder

DIRECTIONS

Preheat oven to 400 degrees. Mix one tablespoon
of olive oil with 1/4 teaspoon garlic powder. Rub
mushrooms evenly with the mixture; place on greased
baking sheet.

Heat one tablespoon of olive oil over medium heat.
Sauté garlic, onion, and roasted red bell peppers for
8–10 minutes or until tender. Season with Italian
seasoning. Add olives and cooked sausage the last two
minutes of cook time.

Spread three tablespoons of pizza sauce on each
mushroom. Evenly layer the sausage and vegetable
mixture, mozzarella, and feta cheese on top of the
mushrooms. Bake for 20 minutes. Turn oven to broil
and broil for 2–3 minutes or until cheese is browned
and bubbly.

serves four

Stromboli SUPREME

Stromboli Supreme calls for wraps vs. a thick dough, making it a healthier alternate to a traditional stromboli. It is easy to make and completely satisfies a stromboli or pizza craving. This is a favorite in our household.

INGREDIENTS

4 wraps (I use Angelic Bakehouse or Food for Life Ezekiel.)

12 pieces pepperoni (I use Applegate Farms.)

1/2 cup mushrooms, diced

1/2 cup green pepper, diced

1/2 cup red onion, diced

1/4 cup black olives, sliced

1 cup pizza sauce

1 cup mozzarella cheese, shredded

1/2 tablespoon olive oil

DIRECTIONS

Preheat oven to 375 degrees. Place wraps on a baking sheet (you may need two sheets). Evenly brush one side of the wraps with olive oil; flip wraps over. Spread 1/4 cup pizza sauce over each wrap. Lay 3 pieces of pepperoni and an equal portion of the mushrooms, green pepper, red onion, black olives, and mozzarella cheese over one side of each wrap. Fold the other side of each wrap over the toppings. Gently press to ensure wraps stay folded. Bake for 18–22 minutes or until cheese has melted and wraps are slightly browned. Let cool for 5 minutes. Slice each wrap into thirds.

Serving Suggestion: Serve with Roasted Broccoli (page 142).

serves four

Greekza PIZZA

The seasoning for the beef on this pizza is reminiscent of traditional Greek flavors. I like to double the meat portion of this recipe and use the leftovers for Greek salads or wraps the following day.

INGREDIENTS

4 wraps (I use Angelic Bakehouse or Food for Life Ezekiel.)

1 lb. ground beef

1 cup garlic hummus

4 pepperoncinis, chopped

1 cup feta cheese, crumbled

1 tablespoon olive oil

1 teaspoon minced garlic

2 teaspoons oregano

1 teaspoon garlic powder

1 teaspoon onion powder

1 teaspoon basil

1 teaspoon paprika

1 teaspoon black pepper

1 teaspoon parsley

1/2 teaspoon thyme

1/2 teaspoon nutmeg

1/2 teaspoon cinnamon

DIRECTIONS

Preheat oven to 400 degrees. Mix all seasoning ingredients together (excluding minced garlic). Heat skillet over medium heat. Add beef and seasoning to skillet. Cook and crumble beef for 8–10 minutes or until cooked throughout. Keep warm.

Mix olive oil with minced garlic. Brush both sides of each wrap with the olive oil and garlic mixture. (You may have leftover olive oil.) Place wraps on a baking sheet (you may need two sheets) and bake for 4–5 minutes on each side or until sightly browned. Remove from oven.

Top each wrap with a 1/4 cup of hummus and an equal portion of the beef, feta, and pepperoncinis. Bake for 4–6 minutes or until hummus and feta are warmed and edges of wraps are browned.

Serving Suggestion: Serve with Greek Salad (page 77). Omit chicken in Greek salad recipe.

serves four

BBQ Chicken
STUFFED SWEET POTATOES

This is my favorite BBQ chicken recipe. It calls for less BBQ sauce than typical BBQ chicken recipes, making it a lower sugar option. The addition of Italian dressing gives it a little bit of zip! Stuffing sweet potatoes with the chicken is a fun twist but it can also be classically served on buns.

INGREDIENTS

1 lb. chicken breast

3/4 cup BBQ sauce (I use Annie's Original.)

1/4 cup Italian dressing (I use Annie's Tuscany Italian.)

1/4 cup low-sodium chicken stock

1 tablespoon Worcestershire sauce

4 small sweet potatoes

1 tablespoon olive oil

1/4 teaspoon salt

1/8 teaspoon pepper

diced avocado, for serving

chopped red onion, for serving

crumbled feta cheese, for serving

DIRECTIONS

Place chicken, BBQ sauce, Italian dressing, Worcestershire sauce, chicken stock, salt, and pepper in greased slow cooker. Cover and cook on high for 3–4 hours or on low for 6–8 hours. Remove chicken; shred and place back in slow cooker. Keep on warm.

Heat oven to 375 degrees. Poke each sweet potato with a fork three times. Rub sweet potatoes with olive oil and place on a baking sheet. Bake for 45–60 minutes or until tender. Remove from oven; let cool.

Split open each sweet potato. Put pressure on both ends to open up the center. Top each sweet potato with BBQ chicken, avocado, red onion, and feta cheese.

serves four

BBQ Chicken
SPAGHETTI SQUASH CASSEROLE

If you like BBQ chicken, you will love this casserole. At first it may sound like a strange recipe, but trust me—it's delicious! It will quickly become a family favorite.

INGREDIENTS

1 large or 2 small spaghetti squash to yield 8 cups of squash

2 cups cooked chicken

1/2 cup red onion, chopped

1 green bell pepper, diced

1 clove garlic, minced

3 eggs, whisked

1 cup cheddar cheese, shredded

1 cup BBQ sauce (I use Annie's Original.)

1 tablespoon BBQ seasoning

1 tablespoon plus 1 teaspoon olive oil, divided

1/4 teaspoon salt

1/8 teaspoon pepper

DIRECTIONS

Preheat oven to 375 degrees. Cut each spaghetti squash in half and scoop out the seeds. Brush squash with 1 teaspoon of olive oil. Place face down on a baking sheet and bake for 45 minutes or until tender; let cool. Gently use a fork to pull the strands of squash away from the rind. Place squash strands in a large bowl. Set aside.

Heat one tablespoon of olive oil over medium heat. Add red onion, garlic, and bell pepper; sauté for 8–10 minutes or until vegetables become slightly tender.

Add sautéed vegetables, cooked chicken, BBQ seasoning, BBQ sauce, eggs, salt, and pepper to spaghetti squash. Gently stir to thoroughly combine. Pour squash into a greased 9x13 baking dish. Top with cheese. Bake at 350 degrees for 30–45 minutes or until ingredients are warmed and cheese has melted and is bubbly.

serves six

Slow Cooker
CHICKEN TACO BAR

This recipe is another winner! It is so easy to prepare and everyone loves it.
I like to set up a "taco bar" and let everyone build their own tacos or taco salads.

INGREDIENTS

2 lbs. chicken breast

16–20 oz. jar of red or green salsa

3 tablespoons Mexican seasoning (page 38)

1/2 teaspoon salt

1/4 teaspoon pepper

Fixin's:

corn shells

shredded lettuce

diced tomato

pepper jack cheese

diced avocado

black olives

black or pinto beans

corn

sour cream

chipotle mayonnaise

DIRECTIONS

Place chicken, salsa, Mexican seasoning, salt, and pepper in a greased slow cooker. Cook on high for 3–4 hours or on low for 6–8 hours. Remove chicken; shred and place back into slow cooker. Keep on warm.

Place all fixin's in separate bowls. Allow everyone to build their own tacos.

Have leftover chicken? Use it for Southwest Salads (page 79), quesadillas, or tostadas.

serves six to eight

Slow Cooker
CILANTRO STEAK FAJITAS

This is such an easy way to enjoy steak tacos. The slow cooker makes the steak very tender. We have this at least once a month in our house. When we have leftover steak, we diced it up and add it to scrambled eggs the next morning.

INGREDIENTS

2 lb. beef tri-tip roast, sliced into 1" thick pieces

1 orange bell pepper, sliced

1 yellow bell pepper, sliced

1 red bell pepper, sliced

1 large yellow onion, sliced

16–20 oz. jar of red salsa

1/2 cup low-sodium beef stock

3 tablespoons Mexican seasoning (page 38)

diced avocado, for serving

corn shells, for serving

sour cream, for serving

fresh cilantro, for serving

DIRECTIONS

Add beef, peppers, onion, salsa, beef stock, and Mexican seasoning to slow cooker; stir to mix well. Cook on low for 8–10 hours. Remove steak; shred and put back into slow cooker. Keep on warm. Serve fajitas in taco shells and top with avocado, sour cream, and cilantro.

serves eight

Cuban
QUESADILLAS

This is a healthier version of a Cuban sandwich. The ham, Swiss, and dill pickles are reminiscent of a traditional Cuban but this version calls for wraps vs. crusty bread, making it a lighter and lower-carb option.

INGREDIENTS

4 wraps (I use Angelic Bakehouse or Food for Life Ezekiel.)

8 pieces ham, sliced thin

4 slices Swiss cheese

12 small dill pickle slices

1 tablespoon plus 1 teaspoon butter, divided

mustard, to taste

DIRECTIONS

Heat 1 teaspoon butter over medium-high heat; swirl pan to coat. Place one wrap in skillet. On one half of the wrap, layer two pieces of ham, one slice of cheese, three pickles, and mustard. Fold opposite side of wrap over toppings. Cook for 4–5 minutes or until bottom side of wrap becomes crisp. Flip; continue to cook for another 4–5 minutes or until both sides of the wrap are crisp and cheese has melted. Repeat steps with the remaining ingredients. Cut each wrap into thirds.

serves four

Tuscan PIZZA

INGREDIENTS

1 chicken breast

1/8 cup pesto

1 thin-crust whole grain pizza crust
(I use Angelic Bakehouse Flatzza.)

1 cup pizza sauce

1 clove garlic, minced

1/4 cup artichoke hearts, diced

1/4 cup Kalamata olives, diced

1/4 cup sweet onion, diced

1 1/2 cups mozzarella cheese, shredded

1/2 cup feta cheese, crumbled

1/2 tablespoon olive oil

1 teaspoon basil

1/4 teaspoon salt

1/8 teaspoon pepper

DIRECTIONS

Preheat oven to 350 degrees. Place chicken in a greased baking dish. Spread pesto over chicken. Cover and bake for 45–60 minutes or until chicken reaches an internal temperature of 165 degrees. Remove from oven; let cool. Dice chicken into small pieces; set aside.

Heat olive oil over medium heat. Sauté garlic, artichokes, olives, and onion for 5–7 minutes or until slightly tender. Season with basil, salt, and pepper.

Spread pizza sauce on pizza crust. Top with sautéed vegetables, diced chicken, and cheese. Bake according to crust package directions.

serves four

Ground Beef TOSTADAS

Tostadas were one of my favorite recipes growing up. My mom knew that everyone in the family would be happy if she made them. They are simple, delicious, and can easily be customized for the pickiest of eaters! (Yes, there was a time when I was a picky eater and I would only eat nachos with cheese or toasted cheese sandwiches.) You can swap chicken for the beef or add additional toppings like corn and black beans.

INGREDIENTS

1 lb. ground beef

1/2 small red onion, diced

1 small red bell pepper, diced

1 tablespoon jalapeño, finely diced

15 oz. can refried beans

1 cup enchilada sauce

1 cup cheese (I like feta and Cody prefers pepper jack.)

8 corn tortillas

3 tablespoons Mexican seasoning, divided (page 38)

1/4 teaspoon salt

1/2 tablespoon olive oil

shredded lettuce, for serving

diced tomato, for serving

diced avocado, for serving

salsa, for serving

sour cream, for serving

DIRECTIONS

Place red onion, red pepper, jalapeño, and ground beef in a pan. Season with two tablespoons of Mexican seasoning. Cook over medium heat until beef is cooked throughout and vegetables are slightly tender. Drain grease. Add enchilada sauce to pan and cook over low heat for 5–10 minutes allowing flavors to meld.

Turn broiler on. Lay tortillas on two baking sheets. Evenly brush both sides of the tortillas with olive oil. Sprinkle tortillas with salt. Broil for 2–3 minutes or until tortillas are just slightly browned and crispy. Remove from oven.

Mix refried beans with one tablespoon of Mexican seasoning. Heat beans according to package directions. Spread a thin layer of refried beans onto each tortilla. Top each tortilla with roughly 1/4 cup ground beef mixture and 1/8 cup cheese. Put tortillas back into oven and broil for 1–2 minutes or until cheese has melted.

Top each tostada with desired amount of lettuce, tomato, avocado, salsa, and sour cream.

serves four

Mexican BOWLS

This is a staple recipe in our house. I love that the base is made from riced cauliflower vs. a traditional rice. The addition of onion, jalapeños, peppers, beans, and corn add many layers of flavor. You can customize this recipe by swapping in another meat for the chicken or adding different vegetables.

INGREDIENTS

1 lb. chicken breast

4 cups riced cauliflower

1/2 small red onion, diced

1 tablespoon jalapeño, finely minced

1 red pepper, diced

1 green pepper, diced

1/2 cup grape tomatoes, sliced in half

1 cup black beans, rinsed and drained

1/2 cup corn

1 cup red or green salsa

3 tablespoons Mexican seasoning, divided (page 38)

2 tablespoons olive oil

1/4 teaspoon salt

1/8 teaspoon pepper

diced avocado, for serving

salsa, for serving

sour cream, for serving

DIRECTIONS

Preheat oven to 400 degrees. Place chicken in a greased baking dish. Season chicken with one tablespoon of Mexican seasoning. Pour salsa over chicken. Cover and bake for 30–45 minutes or until chicken reaches an internal temperature of 165 degrees. Remove from oven. Dice chicken and place in a bowl. Add remaining salsa and juice from baking dish to bowl; mix well with chicken.

Heat olive oil over medium heat. Sauté red onion, jalapeño, and peppers for 8–10 minutes or until tender. Add riced cauliflower, grape tomatoes, beans, and corn. Season with two tablespoon of Mexican seasoning, salt, and pepper. Continue to cook for another 8–10 minutes or until riced cauliflower is tender. Add chicken to vegetable mixture and cook for an additional 2–3 minutes or until well-combined. Serve in bowls. Top with avocado, salsa, and sour cream.

serves four

Cucumber Dill SALMON

This recipe was given to me by a previous co-worker. It was one of the first recipes that I cooked for Cody and after one try he was hooked. It is part of our regular recipe rotation. It feels fancy but is a cinch to cook.

INGREDIENTS

4 pieces salmon

1/2 lemon, for squeezing

1/2 cup mayonnaise

1/2 cup sour cream

1/2 cucumber, peeled, seeded, and diced

2 tablespoons dill, divided

2 tablespoons Dijon mustard

1/8 teaspoon salt

1/8 teaspoon pepper

DIRECTIONS

Preheat oven to 400 degrees. Mix mayonnaise, sour cream, Dijon mustard, 1 tablespoon dill, and cucumber together. Refrigerate for at least 30 minutes. The sauce will be used for serving.

Place salmon in a greased baking dish. Season salmon with 1 tablespoon dill, salt, and pepper. Squeeze lemon over salmon. Bake for 20–25 minutes or until salmon is cooked throughout. Serve salmon with cucumber dill sauce.

Serving Suggestion: Serve with Lemon Parmesan Asparagus (page 151) or Green Bean Almandine (page 147).

serves four

Cracker Crumb
CRUSTED COD

This is my take on a healthier version of fried fish. The Dijon mustard and golden baked cracker crumbs gives a rich, satisfying flavor. I now prefer the light, fresh taste of Cracker Crumb Crusted Cod better than a typical heavily-breaded fried fish.

INGREDIENTS

4 pieces cod

18 butter crackers (I use Late July Classic Rich Crackers or Back to Nature Classic Round Crackers.)

1/4 cup Parmesan cheese, grated

2 tablespoons Dijon mustard

3 tablespoons olive oil

1 teaspoon basil

1/4 teaspoon salt

1/4 teaspoon pepper

1 sandwich-size resealable bag

lemon wedges, for serving

DIRECTIONS

Preheat oven to 425 degrees. Crush crackers in a resealable bag. Add cheese, oil, and basil; shake to combine. Place cod in a greased baking dish; season with salt and pepper. Brush Dijon mustard on the top side of the cod. Press cracker mixture onto the mustard coated side of the fish. Bake for 18–20 minutes or until fish is cooked throughout. Serve with lemon wedges.

Serving Suggestion: Serve with Lemon Parmesan Asparagus (page 151) or Green Bean Almandine (page 147).

serves four

Italian
BEEF

This is a simplified version of a recipe my Aunt Sue shared with me years ago. It really can't get easier than adding two ingredients to a slow cooker! It is a perfect dish to bring to a potluck, serve at a party, or drop off to a friend in need. I enjoy mine as is but you can serve them traditionally on crusty Italian buns.

INGREDIENTS

DIRECTIONS

2–3 lb. shoulder roast

16 oz. jar pepperoncinis

Put roast and entire jar of pepperoncinis (liquid included) into a greased slow cooker. Cook on low for 10–12 hours. Remove beef; shred and put back into slow cooker. Keep on warm.

serves eight

Cody's
GRILLED CHEESEBURGERS

Cody has perfected the cheeseburger. A simple seasoning of salt and pepper allows the flavor of the beef to shine through and the hint of Worcestershire sauce adds a layer of depth. I ask Cody to grill these at least once a week in the summer. I like mine served over lettuce with tomato, onion, and pickles on top but you can serve them traditionally on buns.

INGREDIENTS

1 1/2–2 lbs. ground beef

1 tablespoon plus 1 teaspoon Worcestershire sauce

4 slices cheddar or Swiss cheese

1/4 teaspoon salt

1/8 teaspoon pepper

lettuce, for serving

tomato slices, for serving

red onion slices, for serving

pickle slices, for serving

DIRECTIONS

Remove meat from refrigerator 30–60 minutes before cooking–the closer to room temperature the meat is the more evenly it will cook. Heat grill to medium-high heat. Form four burger patties with the beef. Press a divot in the center of the burger with your index finger and thumb. (Be careful not to poke a hole all of the way through.) This will keep the burgers from shrinking. Rub 1 teaspoon of Worcestershire sauce over each burger. Season burgers with salt and pepper. Grill burgers for 5–7 minutes on each side or until desired degree of doneness is reached. Two minutes before burgers are done cooking, add a slice of cheese to each one. Serve burgers on lettuce and top with tomato, red onion, and pickles.

Serving Suggestion: Serve with Seven Layer Salad (page 76) and Cody's Loaded Hasselback Potatoes (page 149).

serves four

Everyday CHILI

This is my mom's chili recipe and it reminds me of college football season. We have spent many Saturdays throughout the years attending Notre Dame football games and then coming home to enjoy big bowls of chili. For a large crowd, double the recipe and set up a "chili bar" with toppings like cheddar cheese, sour cream, tortilla chips, green onion, and diced avocado.

INGREDIENTS

1 lb. ground beef

1 small yellow onion, chopped

2 garlic cloves, minced

2 15 oz. cans chili beans (I use Westbrae Organic.)

15 oz. can diced tomatoes, undrained

8 oz. can tomato sauce

2 tablespoons chili powder

1 1/2 teaspoons cumin

1/2 teaspoon salt

1/4 teaspoon pepper

DIRECTIONS

In a large pan or soup pot, cook beef, onion, and garlic; drain fat. Stir in remaining ingredients. Bring to a simmer and cook for one hour. The longer it simmers, the better the flavors will develop.

Have leftover chili? Use it to make chili dogs, nachos, or stuffed potatoes.

serves four

Date Night
CHICKEN CORDON BLEU

This is the first meal Cody ever cooked for me. It holds a special place in my heart and I often request it when he and I have an at-home date night! This will always be a meaningful meal for both of us.

INGREDIENTS

4 small pieces chicken breast

4 pieces ham, sliced thin

4 slices Swiss cheese

4 tablespoons Dijon mustard

1 cup panko bread crumbs

1 1/2 teaspoons parsley

1/4 teaspoon salt

1/8 teaspoon pepper

Parmesan cheese, for serving

DIRECTIONS

Preheat oven to 400 degrees. Mix bread crumbs, parsley, salt, and pepper together in a flat dish; set aside. Butterfly chicken. Stuff one piece of ham and one piece of cheese into each chicken breast. Brush each chicken breast with one tablespoon of Dijon mustard. Press each chicken breast into Panko breadcrumb mixture and place in a greased baking dish. (You may have leftover bread crumbs). Bake for 30–45 minutes or until chicken reaches an internal temperature of 165 degrees. Lightly sprinkle with Parmesan cheese.

Serving Suggestion: Serve with Garlic Mashed Cauliflower (page 137) and Green Bean Almandine (page 147).

serves four

Creamy
CHICKEN & QUINOA

When I was a kid, this was one of my favorite meals my mom would make. It is pure comfort food to me. The original recipe is written to use wide egg noodles but over the years I have transitioned to using quinoa instead. It is just as comforting and I feel good about knowing I am getting more nutritional bang for my buck.

INGREDIENTS

1 lb. chicken breast, boiled and chopped

1 small yellow onion, chopped

2 stalks celery, chopped

2 teaspoons garlic, minced

1/2 stick butter

2 12–15 oz. packages cream of chicken soup (I use Pacifica.)

5 cups low-sodium chicken stock, divided

2 cups quinoa, rinsed

1 tablespoon parsley

1/4 teaspoon pepper

DIRECTIONS

Cook quinoa according to package directions substituting chicken stock for water. Set aside.

In a large pan or sauce pot, heat butter over medium heat. Sauté onion, celery, and garlic for 10–12 minutes or until tender. Add chicken, cream of chicken soup, 1/2 cup chicken stock, parsley, and pepper; mix well. Fold in cooked quinoa. Add remaining 1/2 cup chicken stock if you prefer a thinner consistency. Cover and keep on warm until you are ready to serve.

Serving Suggestion: Serve with Roasted Broccoli (page 142).

serves four to six

Cheesy
SLOPPY POTATOES

This is a fun twist on a classic sloppy joe. Kids (and adults) will have fun piling
their potatoes high with sloppy joe mix and broiling them with cheese.

INGREDIENTS

4 small baking potatoes

1 lb. ground beef

1 small sweet onion, finely chopped

8 oz. can tomato sauce

1/4 cup water

1 cup cheddar cheese, shredded

1 tablespoon chili powder

1 tablespoon brown sugar

1 tablespoon olive oil

1/2 teaspoon salt

sour cream, for serving

sliced green onion, for serving

DIRECTIONS

Heat oven to 375 degrees. Poke each potato with a
fork three times. Rub potatoes with olive oil and place
on a baking sheet. Bake for 45–60 minutes or until
tender. Remove from oven; let cool. Turn on broiler to
prepare for last step.

Heat skillet to medium heat. Add beef and onion; cook
for 10–12 minutes or until beef is cooked through;
drain. Stir in chili powder, sugar, and salt; cook for
1 minute, stirring constantly. Add 1/4 cup water
and tomato sauce; bring to a boil and reduce heat to
simmer for 3–5 minutes or until thickened.

Split open each potato. Put pressure on both ends to
open up the center. Fill each potato with beef mixture.
Sprinkle potatoes with cheese. Broil for 2–4 minutes
or until cheese is browned and bubbly. Serve each
potato with sour cream and green onion.

Serving Suggestion: Serve with Seven Layer Salad
(page 76).

serves four

Side Dishes

Basic
CAULIFLOWER RICE

Cauliflower rice is one of my favorite go-to side dishes. I love replacing higher-carb options like rice with a more nutrient-dense and lower-carb option like this. Cauliflower rice is hearty, comforting, and filling.

INGREDIENTS

1 head cauliflower, trimmed and cut into florets

2 tablespoons olive oil

1/4 teaspoon salt

1/8 teaspoon pepper

DIRECTIONS

Place cauliflower florets into a blender. Pulse 4–5 times until cauliflower resembles rice. You may need to do this in batches. Heat olive oil in a pan over medium heat. Sauté riced cauliflower for 8–10 minutes or until tender. Season with salt and pepper.

In a hurry? Look for pre-riced cauliflower at your local grocery store. It can be found in the produce or freezer section. It is sometimes labeled as "cauliflower crumbles."

serves four

Mexican CAULIFLOWER RICE

You can get as creative as you want with this recipe by adding diced bell peppers, beans, or corn!

INGREDIENTS

1 head cauliflower, trimmed and cut into florets

2 tablespoons olive oil

1/2 yellow onion, diced

1/4 cup green onions, sliced

1/8 teaspoon salt

1/8 teaspoon pepper

2 tablespoons Mexican seasoning (page 38)

DIRECTIONS

Place cauliflower florets into a blender. Pulse 4–5 times until cauliflower resembles rice. You may need to do this in batches. Heat olive oil in a pan over medium heat. Sauté yellow onion for 4–5 minutes or until slightly tender. Add cauliflower rice to pan. Season with Mexican seasoning, salt, and pepper. Sauté for 8–10 minutes or until cauliflower is tender. Stir in green onions.

serves four

Asian
CAULIFLOWER RICE

This is one of my favorite side dishes! On nights when time is short, I simply add sautéed shrimp (sauté shrimp in one tablespoon coconut oil and season with salt and pepper) to make this a complete meal.

INGREDIENTS

1 head cauliflower, trimmed and cut into florets

3 tablespoons coconut oil

1 cup broccoli florets, finely chopped

1 cup pea pods

1/2 cup water chestnuts, sliced

2 tablespoons low-sodium tamari or soy sauce

1 tablespoon sesame oil

1 1/2 teaspoons sesame seeds, optional

DIRECTIONS

Place cauliflower florets into a blender. Pulse 4–5 times until cauliflower resembles rice. You may need to do this in batches. Heat coconut oil in a pan over medium heat. Sauté broccoli, pea pods, and water chestnuts for 8–10 minutes or until tender. Add riced cauliflower and sauté for an additional 8–10 minutes or until cauliflower is tender. Remove from heat and add soy sauce and sesame oil. Toss to combine well. Top with sesame seeds if desired.

serves four

Basic SPAGHETTI SQUASH

Spaghetti squash is the new noodle. Spaghetti squash is higher in nutrients and lower in carbohydrates than a typical noodle, making it a healthier option. Plus, it fills you up without weighing you down. Try Basic Spaghetti Squash with Mom's Homemade Italian Meatballs (page 91), Oven-Baked Chicken Parmesan (page 93), Mom's Easy Chicken Cacciatore (page 94), or Slow Cooker Sausage and Peppers (page 95).

INGREDIENTS

2 small to medium or 1 large spaghetti squash

1/2 tablespoon olive oil

pinch of salt

pinch of pepper

DIRECTIONS

Preheat oven to 375 degrees. Cut spaghetti squash in half length-wise, scoop out seeds and discard. Brush flesh side of squash with olive oil. Sprinkle with salt and pepper. Place squash on baking sheet (rind side up) and cook for 45–60 minutes or until done. You should be able to indent the rind with your finger. Take a fork and gently pull apart the strands.

serves four

Basic PESTO ZOODLES

Zoodles are simply zucchini that have been spiralized into noodle form. This is a healthy alternative to pasta noodles. Adding pesto gives the zoodles a touch of flavor. Serve Basic Pesto Zoodles with Baked Pesto Chicken (page 97).

INGREDIENTS

4 zucchini

2 tablespoons olive oil

1/3 cup pesto

1/4 teaspoon salt

1/8 teaspoon pepper

DIRECTIONS

Spiralize zucchini into zoodles. Heat olive oil over medium heat. Sauté zoodles for 6–8 minutes or until slightly tender. Season with salt and pepper. Be careful not to overcook them or they will release a lot of liquid and become mushy. Add pesto; cook for an additional 2–3 minutes or until pesto has coated the zoodles.

serves four

Garlic
MASHED CAULIFLOWER

Mashed cauliflower is a great substitute for mashed potatoes. This recipe is flavorful, creamy, and comforting. We like to serve Garlic Mashed Cauliflower alongside Date Night Chicken Cordon Bleu (page 125). It also pairs great with grilled steak or meatloaf.

INGREDIENTS

1 head cauliflower, trimmed and cut into florets (roughly 8 cups of cauliflower florets)

4 cloves garlic

1/4 cup sour cream

1/4 cup dairy milk, divided

1/4 cup Parmesan cheese, shredded or grated

1 tablespoon parsley

1/2 teaspoon salt

1/4 teaspoon pepper

DIRECTIONS

Boil or steam cauliflower and garlic cloves in medium saucepan for 15 minutes or until tender. Drain cauliflower and put into blender. Add sour cream, 1/8 cup milk, Parmesan cheese, parsley, salt, and pepper. Blend on high until cauliflower resembles mashed potatoes. Add another 1/8 cup milk if a thinner consistency is desired.

serves four

Garlic Parmesan
SAUTÉED ITALIAN VEGETABLES

INGREDIENTS

3 summer squash, diced

3 zucchini, diced

1 yellow onion, diced

2 garlic cloves, minced

2 tablespoons olive oil

1 tablespoon Italian seasoning

1/2 lemon

1/4 cup Parmesan cheese, shaved

1/4 teaspoon salt

1/8 teaspoon pepper

DIRECTIONS

Heat olive oil over medium heat. Sauté squash, zucchini, onion, and garlic for 12–15 minutes or until tender. Season with Italian seasoning, salt, and pepper. Squeeze fresh lemon over vegetables and top with Parmesan cheese.

serves four

Sweet SPROUTS

This is a standby side dish recipe in our house. Cody asks for it at least once every few months. We love serving it alongside of pork or fish. The sweetness from the brown sugar perfectly balances the bitterness of the Brussels sprouts.

INGREDIENTS

2 lbs. Brussels sprouts

3 tablespoons olive oil

1/2 cup chopped walnuts, toasted *

2 tablespoons brown sugar

1/8 teaspoon salt

1/8 teaspoon pepper

DIRECTIONS

Cut stalks off of Brussels sprouts and slice into thirds. Brussels sprouts will resemble shredded lettuce.

Heat olive oil over medium heat. Sauté Brussels sprouts for 12–15 minutes or until slightly tender. Season with salt and pepper. Add walnuts and brown sugar. Cook for an additional 5 minutes or until sugar is caramelized.

*To toast walnuts, place on baking sheet and cook for 4–5 minutes at 400 degrees or until nuts become fragrant.

serves four

Sweet & Savory BRUSSELS SPROUTS

INGREDIENTS

2 lbs. Brussels sprouts

1/2 lb. bacon, cooked and crumbled

1/4 cup chopped walnuts, toasted*

4 Medjool dates, pits removed, and diced

3 tablespoons olive oil

1/8 tablespoon salt

1/8 tablespoon pepper

DIRECTIONS

Cut stalks off of Brussels sprouts and slice into thirds. Brussels sprouts will resemble shredded lettuce.

Heat olive oil over medium heat. Sauté Brussels sprouts for 12–15 minutes or until slightly tender. Season with salt and pepper. Add bacon, toasted walnuts, and dates. Continue to cook for another 5 minutes or until flavors meld.

*To toast walnuts, place on baking sheet and cook for 4–5 minutes at 400 degrees or until nuts become fragrant.

serves four

Roasted
BROCCOLI

Roasting is one of my favorite ways to prepare vegetables. It brings out a deep and earthy flavor. My favorite vegetables to roast are broccoli, cauliflower, carrots, and Brussels sprouts.

. . . .

INGREDIENTS

1 head of broccoli, trimmed and cut into florets

2 tablespoons olive oil

1/4 teaspoon salt

1/8 teaspoon pepper

DIRECTIONS

Preheat oven to 375 degrees. Toss broccoli in olive oil, salt, and pepper. Place on a baking sheet and bake for 30–35 minutes, turning occasionally, or until broccoli is tender and slightly browned.

serves four

Cody's GRILLED VEGETABLES

This is a satisfying side dish that Cody has perfected! We serve this alongside Cody's Grilled Cheeseburgers (page 121).

INGREDIENTS

1 eggplant, ends removed and sliced into 1/2-inch pieces

2 zucchini, ends removed and sliced into 1/2-inch pieces

2 summer squash, ends removed and sliced into 1/2-inch pieces

1/2 cup goat or feta cheese, crumbled

2 tablespoons olive oil

2 tablespoons Worcestershire sauce

1 tablespoon Monterey steak seasoning

DIRECTIONS

Heat grill to medium heat. Rub sliced vegetables with Worcestershire sauce, olive oil, and seasoning. Grill for 8–10 minutes on each side or until slightly charred. Remove from grill and top with cheese.

serves four

Roasted
SWEET POTATOES,
BRUSSELS SPROUTS,
& RED ONION

INGREDIENTS

2 sweet potatoes, peeled and diced

1 lb. Brussels sprouts, stalks removed and sliced in half

1 red onion, roughly chopped

2 tablespoons olive oil

1/4 teaspoon salt

1/8 teaspoon pepper

DIRECTIONS

Preheat oven to 375 degrees. Toss sweet potatoes, Brussels sprouts, and red onion in olive oil, salt, and pepper. Place on a baking sheet and bake for 45 minutes, stirring occasionally, or until sweet potatoes and vegetables are tender and slightly browned.

serves four

Green Bean
ALMANDINE

This side dish pairs perfectly with homestyle recipes like Cracker Crumb Crusted Cod (page 118) and Creamy Chicken and Quinoa (page 127).

INGREDIENTS

2 lbs. green beans, ends trimmed

1/2 cup almond slices

2 tablespoons butter

1/4 teaspoon salt

1/8 teaspoon pepper

DIRECTIONS

Steam green beans for 6–8 minutes or until tender; set aside. Heat butter over medium-high heat. Add almonds and cook for 6–8 minutes, stirring every few minutes, or until almonds are toasted and fragrant. Add green beans to pan. Season with salt and pepper. Toss green beans with buttered almonds until well-combined.

serves four

Cody's Loaded
HASSELBACK POTATOES

INGREDIENTS

4 small baking potatoes

2 tablespoons olive oil

1/4 teaspoon salt

1/8 teaspoon pepper

cheddar cheese, to taste

crumbled bacon, to taste

sour cream, for serving

fresh chives, for serving

DIRECTIONS

Preheat oven to 375 degrees. Cut 1/2-inch slits across the potatoes, stopping just before cutting through. Rub potatoes with olive oil. Gently fan potatoes to ensure olive oil can get in between the slices. Season potatoes with salt and pepper. Bake for 45–60 minutes or until tender. Potato skin should be browned and crispy. Turn oven to broil. Top potatoes with cheese and bacon and broil for 2–4 minutes or until cheese is browned and bubbly. Remove from oven and top with sour cream and chives.

serves four

Lemon Parmesan
ASPARAGUS

This is a simple and delicious recipe. It is one of our go-to weeknight side dishes.

INGREDIENTS

2 lbs. asparagus, ends removed

2 tablespoons olive oil

1/2 lemon, for squeezing

1/4 cup Parmesan cheese, shaved

1/4 teaspoon salt

1/8 teaspoon pepper

DIRECTIONS

Preheat oven to 375 degrees. Rub asparagus with olive oil. Season with salt and pepper. Squeeze 1/2 lemon over asparagus. Bake for for 10–12 minutes or until tender. Top cooked asparagus with Parmesan cheese.

serves four

CHAPTER 11
La Dolce Vita
{THE SWEET LIFE}

Bake these recipes with love and serve for special occasions.

Grandma Bollero's THUMBPRINTS

This is one of my all-time favorite dessert recipes. My Grandma Bollero made them every year for Christmas. Over the years, they have turned into more than just a "Christmas Cookie"—we make them for many other special occasions too. You can change the color of the frosting to match the occasion. My mom made them with pink frosting to serve on the dessert bar at my wedding, and she made them with blue frosting when our first son Bode was born. These cookies will always have a special place in my heart.

INGREDIENTS

Cookies:

1 cup flour

1/2 cup butter, softened to room temperature

1/4 cup brown sugar, packed

1 egg, separated into one egg white and one egg yolk

1/2 teaspoon vanilla

1/4 teaspoon salt

1 cup pecans, finely chopped

Frosting:

4 cups powdered sugar

1/4 cup butter, softened to room temperature

2 egg whites

1–2 tablespoons milk

1 teaspoon vanilla

1/4 teaspoon cream of tartar

food coloring, to your color preference

DIRECTIONS

Preheat oven to 350 degrees. With a mixer, combine brown sugar, butter, vanilla, and egg yolk in a medium bowl. Stir in flour and salt. In a separate bowl, whisk egg white with a fork. Shape dough into 1-inch balls and dip in egg white; roll in pecans. Place on an ungreased cookie sheet. Gently press thumb into center of each cookie to make a divot, being careful not to go through. Bake for 10–12 minutes or until lightly browned. Place cookies on wax or parchment paper to cool.

With a mixer, mix all of the frosting ingredients together. Fill each cookie with 1/2–1 teaspoon of frosting.

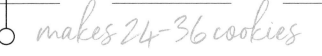

makes 24–36 cookies

Mom's Chocolate TEXAS SHEET CAKE

My mom has been making this recipe for as long as I can remember. It is one of our family's favorite desserts. She classically serves it with chocolate frosting but you could also put sprinkles or nuts on top. A scoop of vanilla ice cream never hurt a piece of Mom's Chocolate Texas Sheet Cake either!

INGREDIENTS

Base:

2 cups flour plus more for flouring pan

2 cups sugar

1 cup margarine

1/2 cup sour cream

1 cup water

2 large eggs

3 tablespoons cocoa powder

1 tablespoon baking soda

1 teaspoon vanilla

1/2 teaspoon salt

butter, for greasing pan

Frosting:

4 cups powdered sugar

1/2 cup margarine

5 tablespoons milk

4 tablespoons cocoa powder

1 tablespoon vanilla

DIRECTIONS

Preheat oven to 350 degrees. Put flour, baking soda, sugar, and salt in a mixing bowl. In a saucepan mix and melt margarine, water, and cocoa powder. Pour margarine mixture over dry ingredients. Add sour cream, eggs, and vanilla. Mix well. Pour into a greased and floured 16x12x1-inch pan. Bake for 20–30 minutes or until a fork inserted comes out clean.

As soon as you pull out the cake, make the frosting. In a saucepan, bring margarine, cocoa, and milk to a boil; stir continuously. Turn to low and add powdered sugar and vanilla; continue to stir until smooth. Pour over warm cake. Let cool completely; store in refrigerator.

Tip: Look for margarine that does not contain hydrogenated or partially-hydrogenated oil.

makes 24-36 squares

Mom's GRASSHOPPER BROWNIES

When my birthday rolls around, this is usually my request! It's a quick and easy recipe that satisfies a sweet tooth. I usually freeze one or two for when a "grasshopper brownie" hankering hits!

INGREDIENTS

1 package of brownie mix (I use Annie's Organic Double Chocolate.)

4 cups powdered sugar

3 oz. cream cheese

1/4 cup plus 2 tablespoons butter

3 tablespoons milk

1 teaspoon vanilla

1/4 teaspoon peppermint extract

green food coloring

2 oz. Baker's chocolate

DIRECTIONS

Cook brownie mix according to package directions; let completely cool. Mix cream cheese, 1/4 cup butter, milk, vanilla, and peppermint extract together. Add a few drops of food coloring to produce a mint green color. Spread frosting on top of the brownies. Melt Baker's chocolate and 2 tablespoons of butter together; drizzle over frosting. Chill until ready to serve. Store in refrigerator.

makes 24 brownies

Aunt Sue's
PEANUT BUTTER CRINKLES

This is my favorite cookie recipe of my Aunt Sue's. She makes them every year for Christmas and it is the first cookie I grab off of the tray!

INGREDIENTS

2 1/2 cups flour, unsifted

1 cup margarine, softened to room temperature

1 cup peanut butter

1 cup sugar plus more for rolling dough

1 cup brown sugar, firmly packed

2 eggs

1 teaspoon vanilla

1 teaspoon baking powder

1 teaspoon baking soda

1 teaspoon salt

14 oz. bag Hershey Kisses, unwrapped

DIRECTIONS

Preheat oven to 350 degrees. In a mixing bowl, beat the margarine, peanut butter, 1 cup of sugar, brown sugar, eggs, and vanilla together. At a slow speed, mix in the flour, baking powder, baking soda, and salt. Shape into 1-inch balls and roll in sugar. Place balls 2-inches apart on ungreased cookie sheets. Bake for 12–15 minutes or until browned. Immediately press Hershey kiss into center of cookie; let cool. Store in airtight container for up to six days.

Tip: Look for margarine made without hydrogenated or partially-hydrogenated oils.

makes 45-60 cookies

PEANUT BUTTER CUP COOKIES

My mother-in-law, Robin, makes this cookie recipe for holidays and special celebrations throughout the year. She knows how much I love them and now calls them "The Gina Cookie!" How can you go wrong with the yummy combination of chocolate and peanut butter?

INGREDIENTS

1 1/4 cups flour

1/2 cup butter, softened to room temperature

1/2 cup peanut butter

1/2 cup white sugar

1/2 cup brown sugar

1 egg

1 teaspoon vanilla

1/2 teaspoon baking soda

1/2 teaspoon baking powder

1/4 teaspoon salt

sugar, for rolling

24 miniature peanut butter cups, unwrapped

DIRECTIONS

Preheat oven to 350 degrees. In a bowl, combine flour, baking soda, baking powder, and salt; set aside. With a mixer, combine butter, peanut butter, sugars, egg, and vanilla together in a large bowl. Add flour mixture and combine. Chill dough for one hour or until firm enough to form balls. Roll dough into 1-inch balls, roll in sugar, and place in mini muffin tins. (Optional to use liners.) Bake for 8–10 minutes or until slightly browned; remove from oven. Press peanut butter cups into the middle of cookies; let cool.

makes 24 cookies

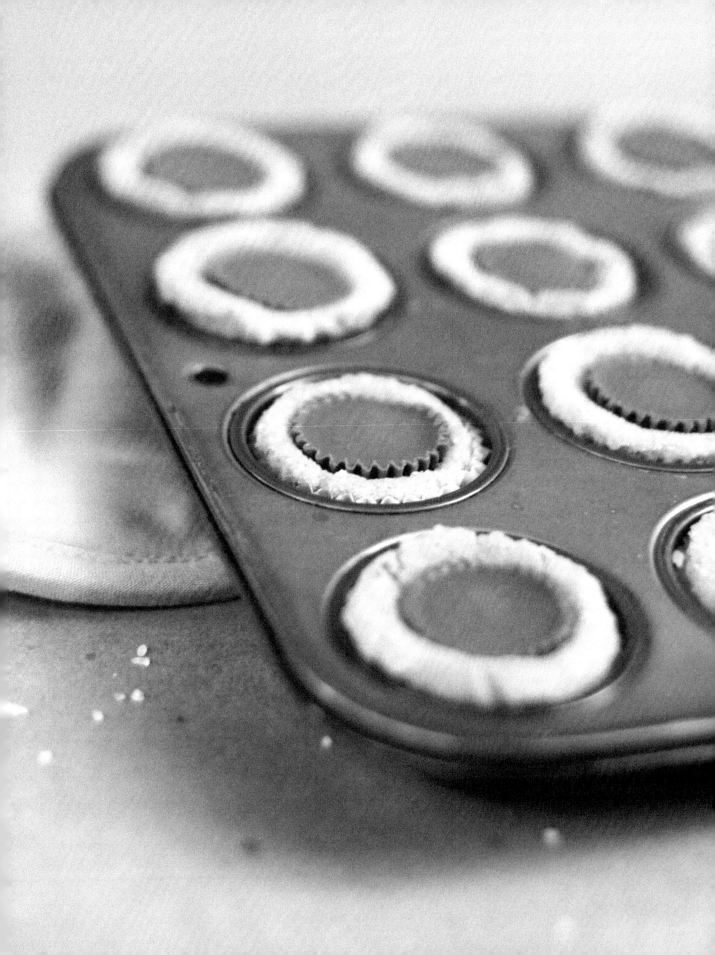

Robin's
CRANBERRY WHITE CHOCOLATE CHIP COOKIES

Cody's mom would send these cookies to him while he was at Indiana University (IU). The cranberries and white chocolate chips made them the perfect red and white IU cookie. They quickly became his favorite and he still lights up to this day when she drops off a batch. Go Hoosiers!

INGREDIENTS

2 1/4 cups flour

3/4 cup sugar

3/4 cup brown sugar

2 eggs

1 cup butter, softened

12 oz. package white chocolate chips

1 cup dried cranberries

1 teaspoon vanilla

1 teaspoon salt

1 teaspoon baking soda

zest of 1 orange

DIRECTIONS

Preheat oven to 350 degrees. Mix flour, salt, and baking soda together; set aside. With a mixer, combine butter, eggs, vanilla, sugars, and orange zest together. Add dry ingredients; mix. Stir in white chocolate chips and dried cranberries. Using a teaspoon, drop cookies onto baking sheets. Bake for 8–10 minutes or until bottom of cookies are slightly browned.

makes 24-36 cookies

Jerry's CHRISTMAS CARAMELS

These caramels are a labor of love but so worth the time. My father-in-law, Jerry, has made them his Christmas specialty. What a treat it is to unwrap one and enjoy it!

INGREDIENTS

2 cups light corn syrup

14 oz. can sweetened condensed milk

1 1/2 cups 2% dairy milk

1 cup whipping cream

1 cup butter plus more for coating baking dish

4 cups sugar

2 teaspoons vanilla

wax paper, cut in 5-inch squares

sea salt, optional

DIRECTIONS

In a 6-quart Dutch oven or pot, combine sugar, corn syrup, condensed milk, milk, whipping cream, and 1 cup of butter. Heat over medium heat and occasionally stir with a wooden spoon until mixture comes to a boil. Then, clip a candy thermometer to side of the pan, and stir constantly until mixture reaches 240 degrees. This will take 45–60 minutes. Remove from heat and add vanilla. Pour into buttered 9x13 baking dish. Do not scrape the edges of the pan as it will become too sugary. Optional to lightly sprinkle with sea salt. Let cool and set overnight. (It does not need to be refrigerated.) Cut into 1-inch squares and wrap in wax paper.

makes 75-100 caramels

Grandma Bollero's
MILLION DOLLAR FUDGE

My Grandma Bollero made this recipe every Christmas–it was a combined effort as my Grandpa always got the job of stirring. In recent years, my mom has taken over the tradition. It never disappoints and brings back the best memories. My personal tradition is to put a few pieces in the freezer for those times when only "Grandma's Fudge" will satisfy.

INGREDIENTS

4 1/2 cups sugar

12 oz. can evaporated milk

2 tablespoons butter plus more for coating baking dish

3, 4 oz. bars German sweet chocolate

16 oz. marshmallow creme

12 oz. semi-sweet chocolate morsels

pinch of salt

DIRECTIONS

In a large bowl, break German chocolate into small pieces. Add marshmallow creme and semi-sweet chocolate; set aside.

In a saucepan, combine sugar, evaporated milk, butter, and salt. Bring to a boil; stir constantly for six minutes.

Gradually pour boiling mixture over chocolate and marshmallow creme mixture. Stir until chocolate has melted. Pour into a buttered 9x13 pan. Let cool on the counter for two hours. Refrigerate for a minimum of 4–6 hours before cutting. Cut into 1-inch pieces.

makes 75-100 pieces

Chapter 12

FOOD FOR THOUGHT

LOOKING FOR A TOTAL FOOD LIFESTYLE TRANSFORMATION?

Through B Present Studio, I have developed a 21 Day Transformation (21DT) program designed for those who want to make healthy, sustainable changes to their food lifestyle.

. . . .

THE PROGRAM INCLUDES:

- 65 recipes plus snack list, smoothie guide, and indulgences
- Grocery shopping guide
- Dining out guide
- Customizable meal planner, exercise log, and results tracker
- Daily support through an online accountability group
- Unlimited Barre On Demand

RESULTS YOU CAN EXPECT:

- Healthy weight loss
- Balanced food choices
- Improved meal planning
- More cooking at home
- Less money spent on groceries
- Reduced sugar intake
- Elimination of artificial ingredients
- Gained nutrition knowledge
- Inches lost
- Decreased belly bloating
- More energy
- Less fatigue
- Better sleep
- More confidence

Please visit *21daytransformation.com* **for more information, sample recipes, and to register.**

21 DAY
TRANSFORMATION

REVIEWS & RECOMMENDATIONS

Thank you for such an awesome, well-rounded program that works! The 21DT helped me to eliminate unnecessary snacking throughout the day and also helped me with portion control. I am approaching my 42nd birthday and I have never felt better inside and out! I have lost 10 lbs, my pants are looser, and I no longer have the "muffin top" that I hated! My husband is down 17 lbs and was able to tighten his belt by two loop holes! Thank you again for such an amazing program. It was a lot of fun and the recipes were spot on! .... *jeanette*

Gina did a FANTASTIC job putting this program together. The 21DT was comprehensive and flexible, the food was really good, and the lists for restaurant meal suggestions, emergency frozen dinners, and grocery products really sets you up for success. It is very clear - a TON of work went into developing this program, and it is well worth the participation price—an extraordinary value. The e-book contains a treasure trove of information. I will continue to use the recipes forever. I plan to continue the program for another month on my own—I genuinely enjoyed it! .... *bridget*

I am happy to report that since starting the 21DT, I haven't had a Diet Coke in three weeks, have completely cut processed foods from my diet, and have lost 8 lbs! I am confident that I will remain much more mindful about what I put into my body. Progress, not perfection! Thank you Gina! ...... *jenny*

The 21DT has changed so much for me. I feel better physically and mentally. My husband and I have been able to follow the meal plan and an exercise plan together consistently for the first time in my life. Since starting this program, I have lost 13.1 lbs. and 4 inches around my waist. Thank you Gina for sharing your knowledge of nutrition, delicious meals, and constant encouragement. It's safe to say, I am a VERY HAPPY CUSTOMER! .... *leslie*

I have struggled for years with my diet and weight and I have finally found something that works! The 21DT has been a game changer for me. I absolutely have loved all the recipes! My husband and I have created healthy habits around drinking more water, correct portion sizes, and meal planning. I feel very confident I will be able to continue this lifestyle for years to come! The bonus is that I lost 7 lbs. and 4 inches! *ashley*
....

WANT MORE RECIPES?

If you enjoyed the recipes in this cookbook and want access to more easy, quick, and family-friendly recipes, please sign up for my newsletter at:

ginaschade.com.

YOU CAN ALSO FOLLOW ME AT:

 *facebook.com/gina.simeri*

@ginaschade

LOOKING FOR MORE RESOURCES?

The following list is a collection of my favorite books, cookbooks, and podcasts. I hope that you can gain as much inspiration from them as I have.

BOOKS/COOKBOOKS:

100 Days of Real Food and *100 Days of Real Food Fast and Fabulous* by Lisa Leake
Against all Grain and *Meals Made Simple* by Danielle Walker
Eating Purely by Elizabeth Stein
Eat Fat, Get Thin by Dr. Mark Hyman
Eat the Yolks by Liz Wolfe
I Quit Sugar by Sarah Wilson
Practical Paleo by Diane Sanfilippo
The Dude Diet by Serena Wolf

PODCASTS:

Balanced Bites by Diane Sanfilippo and Liz Wolfe
Fed and Fit by Cassy Joy Garcia
House Call by Dr. Mark Hyman

Spread The Love

Thank you so much for inviting me into your kitchen. I hope this cookbook inspired you to cook more at home, step out of your comfort zone, and spend a little extra time around the table with your loved ones. If you enjoyed this book and resonated with the 90/10 Life message, please consider leaving a positive review on Amazon. The more positive reviews, the more others will be inspired to get their aprons dirty and serve their family healthy and delicious meals too!

Chapter 13

ABOUT THE AUTHOR

Gina is a wellness coach at B Present Studio and also the creator of the 21 Day Transformation program. She attended the Institute for Integrative Nutrition and is certified through the American Association of Drugless Practitioners. Before working as a wellness coach, she spent seven years working as a Registered Technologist, with a specialization in Mammography. She also has a Bachelors of Science in Business Administration from Central Michigan University. She has always had a special passion for health.

Throughout Gina's training at the Institute for Integrative Nutrition, she studied over 100 different dietary theories, lifestyle management techniques, and innovative coaching methods with some of the world's top health and wellness experts. Her teachers included Dr. Andrew Weil, Director of the Arizona Center for Integrative Medicine; Dr. Deepak Chopra, leader in the field of mind-body medicine; Dr. David Katz, Director of Yale University's Prevention Research Center; Dr. Walter Willett, Chair of Nutrition at Harvard University; Geneen Roth, bestselling author and expert on emotional eating; and many other leading researchers and nutrition authorities.

Her education has equipped her with extensive knowledge in holistic nutrition, wellness coaching, and preventative health. Drawing on her skills and knowledge, she works with clients to help them make lifestyle changes that produce real and lasting results.

Seeing how making small changes positively impacted her own life, she is inspired to share this gift with others. When Gina is not working, you will find her spending time with her family, experimenting in the kitchen, or soaking up the sunshine.

REFERENCES

1. USDA. "Understanding the USDA Organic Label." Accessed June 23, 2017. https://www.usda.gov/media/blog/2016/07/22/understanding-usda-organic-label

2. AHA. "Added Sugars." Last modified February 1, 2017. http://www.heart.org/HEARTORG/HealthyLiving/HealthyEating/Nutrition/Added-Sugars_UCM_305858_Article.jsp#.WU14L1Pyu1s

CPSIA information can be obtained
at www.ICGtesting.com
Printed in the USA
LVOW06*1444141117
556249LV00026B/188/P